TRENDS TRANSFORMING SOUTH AFRICA

TRENDS TRANSFORMING SOUTH AFRICA

INSIGHTS, INFORMATION, AND IDEAS

Compiled and edited by
TONY MANNING

1991

JUTA & CO, LTD

D753

CONTENTS

PART ONE: A COMPLEX PICTURE

PART TWO: VISIONS OF THE FUTURE

Part One
A COMPLEX PICTURE

INTRODUCTION

The term "the new South Africa" is now used so often that it has become almost meaningless. This book is a modest attempt to outline some of the issues that lie ahead of us.

Any time of rapid, discontinuous change presents both threats and opportunities. The world is in the process of painful transition and South Africa is undergoing its own upheaval. Now, as we race into the closing decade of the 20th Century, surprise is the only thing we can be sure of.

But surprises shouldn't get all our attention. We should heed the warning of Robert Ornstein and Paul Erlich in their book *New World New Mind*, that

"the most important 'defaults' of the human mind are to look for discrepancies in the world, to ignore what is going on constantly, and to respond quickly to sudden shifts, to emergencies, to scarcity, to the immediate and personal, to 'news.'"[1]

Certainly, some things do occur all of a sudden, which demand our immediate attention. But other changes unfold over a long period; they give plenty of notice that they're coming.

Take, for instance, demographics. We've been talking about the rapid growth of South Africa's black population for years. Should we be so surprised now, that it really is happening?

Or consider the environmental issue. Conservationists have warned for years that we're destroying the planet. Why are we suddenly paying attention?

The reason we're so slow to sit up, take note, and start doing something, is that our attention gets hijacked by flash events.

1 Robert Ornstein and Paul Ehrlich, *New World New Mind*, Doubleday 1989

The here-and-now makes headline news; who cares about something that might hurt us 20 or 30 years down the line?

But two or three decades ahead is where we have to look. That might be a long time in the life of an individual, but it's a mere blip in the scheme of things. And many responses will take that long to prepare.

On February 2, 1990, State President FW de Klerk put 42 years of apartheid ideology behind him and gave South Africans a new sense of possibilities. He closed a door on the past and opened a new door to the future.

In July, De Klerk spelled out his vision of the future in an interview with Hugh Murray, publisher of *Leadership*. He talked of "full participation for all" . . . of "a vibrant economy" . . . of "a South Africa which offers hope for all its people" . . . of South Africa "becoming an international role player because of the leadership role which history has carved out for us on a continent facing many problems."

When he visited US President George Bush in September, De Klerk went to great lengths to assure the world that the move away from apartheid was irreversible. There was no turning back. We were now all partners in designing the future.

He also went out of his way to assure President Bush that South Africans now embraced the values that Americans had been proud of for so long. *What a radical shift!*

What does all this mean?

What will the "new South Africa" look like?

Will it be the kind of utopia described in the Freedom Charter?

Can we build on the huge pool of goodwill that has survived every kind of assault? Can this possibly become a multi-racial democracy in which differences in race, gender, religion, or political belief are tolerated and accommodated . . . where the rule of law and a bill of rights provide a framework for fair behaviour . . . where people can speak their minds, move about freely and safely, associate with whomever they choose — and vote the way they wish?

Today, anything is possible. The future is a matter of choice, not chance. We get what we expect. We are where we are today because of decisions we took or did not take sometime in the past. When the year 2000 comes around, we'll be somewhere else — not by chance, not by accident, but because of the decisions we take or do not take today.

These are turbulent, disturbing times. Times of excitement and of hope — but also of shock, fear, and despair. Making the most of them will require more guts than many people have. It'll also demand a willingness to make bold leaps of faith . . . to commit resources we do not have to a future we cannot see . . . to open our minds to new ideas and our hearts to people who only recently were "on the other side."

There can be no doubt that painful adjustments will be needed in virtually every aspect of our lives. This beloved country has earned a shocking reputation in the global community. The National Party's bungling programmes of social engineering will surely go down in history as some of the more dreadful examples of man's inhumanity to man.

Responsibility for the future thus lies heavily on each of our shoulders. Each of us has both a say and a stake in the outcome. So we owe it to ourselves, and to those around us, to think carefully about what that "new South Africa" should offer. The future can be what we choose it to be.

Businessmen have a particularly important role to play in shaping the new South Africa. Business organisations are today the most important social arena. They're the one place where people of various races and with different values and views come together on a daily basis with a single purpose: to create wealth.

To create an organisation's future, four "drivers of strategy" must be considered. They are (1) available resources; (2) management's ambitions — their "vision of the future"; (3) their assumptions about how the world around them will change; and (4) their personal values (see the diagram on the following page).

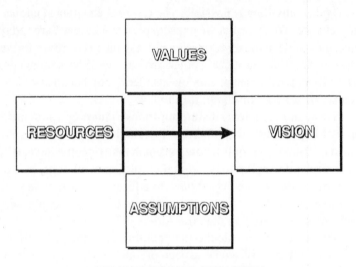

THE DRIVERS OF STRATEGY

When managers think about their organisation's future, they usually start from where they are — in other words, by taking stock of their current resources. They weigh up their strengths and weaknesses to give them a sense of what their possibilities might be.

Because they tend to look inwards before they look outwards, and because they want to keep risks to a manageable level, they often are conservative about their aims. What's more, with things changing so fast around them, and the environment so complex and unpredictable, many managers are loath to spell out their dreams in any detail. They have no real vision of the future. They manage incrementally, one step at a time, one day at a time.

The vision you have of the future hinges on your assumptions. On how you think the future will turn out. It also depends on your values — what you believe in, the principles that guide your behaviour, and what you expect from life.

Assumptions underpin the process of planning. They deserve a good deal of attention. In fact, they get precious little. One reason is that we prefer certainty to uncertainty; and if one thing is certain it's that some of our assumptions will be way off the mark. A second reason is, as one senior executive put it: "I'm too worried about next *week* to think about next year!"

Without giving your assumptions some thought, however, it's virtually impossible to plan sensibly. And why is it that we're quite prepared to lay out assumptions in certain circumstances, and not in others?

For example, if you intend buying a house, you want answers to certain key questions: What's happening to house prices? Are interest rates rising or falling — and how are they likely to behave in the next few years? Which area is likely to give you the best return? Will a road cut through your property sometime in the future? What kinds of neighbours can you expect because of political change?

Of course, you're going to be wrong about some or all of these issues. The best you can do is reduce your risk by thinking about them.

Managers need to go through the same process. And of course, they, too, will make mistakes when they create scenarios of the future. But chances are they'll make fewer, less serious errors, if they at least try to create a snapshot of the future.

One organisation which is extremely concerned about the future is the Building Industries Federation South Africa. The Executive Director, Neil Fraser, readily saw the benefits in encouraging the debate. So BIFSA's 85th annual Congress, held in Durban in October 1990, offered the ideal platform to get the views of a number of leading experts in a wide range of fields.

This book is a record of what they said. Its purpose is to help you think about the problems and opportunities that lie ahead. It offers a variety of insights that will be of interest to every South African.

The opinions expressed are the personal views of the contributors, not BIFSA's, mine (except in the chapter I contributed), or the publisher's.

As Editor of this volume, I'd like to personally thank all who contributed to its success: Neil Fraser, of course, for his encouragement, energy, and leadership. Tony Peepall and Margaret Anderson for burning the midnight oil to make the congress such a success — and Margaret for organising the speakers and chasing them for their papers. Norman Hanna for the cover design. And, of course, the speakers, who made the congress and who make this book what it is. The whole project has been a lot of fun. I hope it helps you realise your dreams in the new South Africa.

Tony Manning
Johannesburg
December 1990

Chapter One
THE BIG PICTURE

DR CONRAD STRAUSS

Dr Conrad Strauss is one of South Africa's most
prominent business leaders, and foremost
visionaries. An economics graduate, he joined the
Standard Bank of South Africa Limited as a
management trainee in 1963, and was appointed
Managing Director just 15 years later. In 1985 he
was appointed Group Managing Director of
Standard Bank Investment Corporation, a position
he holds today. Although his name is synonymous
with banking, his active interest and influence is
felt in many other areas. He is Trustee of the
Poliomyelitis Research Foundation, Chairman of
the South African Institute of International Affairs,
Governor of the University of the Witwatersrand
Foundation, Governor of the Urban Foundation,
and a member of the State President's Economic
Advisory Council. He was named Marketing Man
of the Year by the Institute of Marketing
Management in 1989.

It is clear to all of us, I think, that we are moving into a new, different, and, in many ways, more challenging business environment. Some of the changes are already becoming apparent. Some have not yet emerged.

How successful we are will affect not only South Africa but the whole sub-continent. This country is by far the biggest economic power in the region, and there is no reason why that dominance should not be maintained or even increased. In the long term, therefore, South Africa has not only an exciting future, but also one that is critical to the welfare of a larger region with close to 100 million people.

But our immediate prospects are clouded. Our path is likely to be bumpy for some time, and we must expect setbacks. Nor should we look for clear-cut answers to our questions. In a society changing as fast as this one, a coherent vision of the future will take some time to emerge. Nevertheless, we can make some basic judgments.

One is that the economy is now in a recession and there is little chance of a significant early improvement.

It seems to me, though, that however much present monetary and fiscal policies may hurt, the case for maintaining a tight rein on the economy is irrefutable. It's true that external political pressures are easing as a result of the new domestic political initiatives. This is to be welcomed, but two main monetary related problems still face us.

First, our inflation rate is higher than that of most of our main trading partners. This weakens the value of the rand in terms of other currencies, which in turn makes it more difficult to reduce domestic inflation.

Second, there is the burden of our foreign debt repayment commitments together with our low currency reserves. If we let the brakes off the economy too much too soon, there would be serious consequences for our future well-being.

It is important, then, that we should put the economy on a sound footing now, before new constitutional structures are in place. A new, democratically elected government will be under immediate pressure from its wider constituency to correct existing imbalances in our society by, in effect, throwing money at particularly important problem areas.

If the new government should give way to pressures of this kind, it would seriously affect economic stability.

Back to basics

We are into a period of fundamental and rapid social change. In such times, the first aim of economic management should be maintain a stable and predictable economic policy climate. This means that we should continuously stress our long-term interests and the importance of sound economic fundamentals.

These fundamentals dictate, among other things, that we maintain positive real interest rates and that we balance increases and expenditure in one area by cuts in another — or by corresponding increases in income. Where possible, we should phase out subsidies, or at least reject the hidden subsidies that are major causes of distortion in the economy.

If there is to be a subsidy, the public is entitled to know its extent and its real cost.

We'll get the economic system we choose

Businessmen will have to become much more proactive in helping to shape the future regulatory environment, particularly in the next two to three years. It will not be enough simply to be a good corporate citizen; society demands much more of us than that. If we do not take some firm initiatives, we may well find a very deficient economic system foist upon us. The case for a more practical and efficient one has gone by default.

Business has been explicitly asked, by Mr Mandela among others, to enter the debate on the nature of our future economic system. If we fail to respond, we have only ourselves to blame when our views are not taken into account. The shape of a future South Africa will be moulded by political parties, not all of whom are well-informed or experienced in economic and commercial matters.

Politicians shape the environmental framework within which you and I have to conduct our business. Businessmen will not sit at the negotiating table, but they should come forward with their resources, information banks, and analytical skills, to engage those political parties that are involved in the negotiation process. This can be done by individuals, by companies, or by organised business.

Correcting the imbalances

In shaping a new economic system, we start from the basis that successive governments have built social and economic structures that concentrated wealth and power in the hands of a small minority. Resources were not allocated, and wealth was not distributed, so as to meet the needs of the great bulk of the population. There is too great a gap between the housing, education, and social security facilities of different sections of the population. We must set out to correct this inequity by allowing wealth to permeate the economy more evenly.

This emphatically does not mean that the first aim of economic policy should be, as the current catch phrase puts it, "the redistribution of income." We know from experience worldwide that a policy based only on redistribution would lead to disaster. Instead, we must make our main objective the *creation of wealth.*

If government is to have enough income to channel substantial funds to desirable social ends, we must reach higher and sustainable levels of real increases in national product. This means a growth imperative.

The need for a growing tax base

Government, through the budget, will be the most significant single redistributor of wealth — but only if it has a growing income or tax base from which to do so.

If a future government should seek to extract more income from a static tax base in order to do its redistribution job, it would kill the proverbial golden goose.

In helping to shape our future economy, the business community must recognise the importance of regional and international issues.

While we should not look abroad for much relief from the short-term pressures on the economy, South Africa, under a much more democratic government, will enjoy renewed international credibility. We can anticipate some reintegration into the international financial system, with improved access to capital markets and renewed foreign investment. This alone would improve our domestic economic position.

South Africa's regional role

South Africa is the power-house of the sub-continent, and has a part to play in the development of the whole continent of Africa.

Over the long term this could be an advantage, because it would expose the economy to external competition. All the most successful economies stay open to world trade. Studies by the World Bank, in particular, show that countries choosing inward-looking, protectionist systems fail.

South Africa already has a relatively open economy and we must do what we can not merely to preserve it, but to open it even further, particularly to trade with the rest of Africa. There simply is no other way to create more wealth.

A further condition for success is that we bring our day-to-day conduct of business more into line with the realities of the new South Africa.

The inequalities of the past cannot be corrected by government action alone. It is pointless to spend time allocating culpability for our present situation. Regardless of who got us into this predicament, we all have to accept our share of responsibility for getting out of it. It is obvious to me that some form of affirmative action programme will be an essential weapon for successful businesses in the short to medium term. The key will be human resource management.

Investing in people

Perhaps the biggest single determinant of the economic growth of any country is the educational level of its workforce.

In South Africa, the inadequate training of most black people — from artisans to middle managers — is a major constraint on our development. Together with sometimes unrealistic expectations of promotion and responsibility, this holds potential for serious conflict unless steps are taken by employers to redress the imbalance.

It would be quite inappropriate to promote incompetent people on the basis of racially determined criteria. That has happened in South Africa for far too long. It should be part of every manager's brief to make all staff worthy of greater responsibility, and to clear the way for their advancement.

The issue of correcting imbalances goes well beyond the workplace, into the broader social ills of South Africa. Poor housing, low standards of medical treatment, inadequate infrastructure and communications, are all matters that sooner or later will impinge on business operations and will demand management action.

For business to take corrective action in such matters may be new to most South Africans, but it is certainly not a new idea in itself.

Provision of housing, health care, pre-primary schooling, and other social services, has been a feature of business operations in several leading manufacturing countries since the turn of the century.

If we accept that it is both desirable and necessary for business to create a favourable environment for future expansion, it follows that management will have to look hard at its spending in the broader social responsibility area. Many South African companies already spend more in this way than their counterparts overseas. But they'll have to do even more. It is in their long-term interests to do so. Such expenditure today will help create the right environment for business expansion tomorrow.

Encouraging small business

One area that should be stressed is the promotion of small business. There are two reasons for this.

First, a growing small business sector is the best way to spread the benefits of the market system beyond the white elite. Second, job creation is one of our major priorities, and small business enterprises have proved an excellent generator of employment.

One immediate way in which small business can be encouraged is for management to explore ways and means of directing purchasing programmes towards small businesses and those on the fringe of the formal sector.

The new consumer

Marketing and production policies will have to change in the new economic environment. We can expect much greater government expenditure in areas such as housing, education, and social services, with commensurate savings in areas such as military budgets.

The change will have a significant impact on the pattern of total consumer spending. More money is likely to be spent on everyday consumer goods. These goods are also likely to form the basis of a rapidly expanding regional trade in manufactures.

Among other major developments, there will be a dramatic increase in the proportion of South Africans living in towns and cities. The urbanisation process will be mirrored by significant changes in rural land ownership and patterns of habitation. The advent of black small farmers will bring with it a new set of demands on businesses in the agricultural sector.

Needed: new ideas

I would argue that existing institutions in both the state and private sectors could be re-moulded to meet the new challenges. Among public institutions, both the Industrial Development Corporation and the Land Bank, in particular, could assume new roles relatively easily. In the private sector, many industries have structures and skills which would be readily adaptable to new conditions.

The financial services industry, among others, will have to redefine its methods. Special attention will have to be given to ways of improving access to credit for small business, and to revising products and delivery systems for the particular and growing demands of the black market.

Man vs. machine

A further shift in emphasis is likely to be towards labour-intensive production systems, as a result of both the high cost of capital and the need for job creation. Much of South Africa's past reliance on capital-intensive methods happened for essentially political reasons.

Encouraged by low and often negative interest rates, and artificially high labour costs, management opted for capital-intensive methods. Successive governments had distorted the labour market. Labour mobility was limited, which reduced price competition. Job reservation gave workers of particular racial groups special privileges, thus creating a high-cost labour elite. Finally, there was undue concentration on high-technology areas as part of a search for military and economic self-sufficiency. This, in turn, caused heavy resources to be invested in developing skills that could be only narrowly deployed.

We can expect these conditions to fall away. It will then make economic sense to look for opportunities to exploit more labour-intensive production techniques in certain industries.

Whether this proves successful will depend on relative factor costs. Much will depend on the conduct of trade unions. If they have the ear of a new government, political measures might keep labour costs high relative to other factors of production.

Labour unrest, fomented in the process of creating a labour aristocracy of union members, could cause serious production disruptions in the short term. In the long run, it would drive up labour costs and lead management — if they invest at all — to a renewed search for capital-intensive systems. This would obviously be to the detriment of those excluded from the job market.

The First World component of the economy cannot and will not provide all the jobs we need. It would be a mistake to put further resources into that element at the expense of extending economic activity to a greater proportion of the population.

New demands on our leaders

The picture of South Africa that is slowly emerging is of a country undergoing fundamental changes in its political, social, and economic systems. This will happen within a very short period.

Unfortunately, economic circumstances are not likely to be particularly favourable in the transition phase, and this will place heavy demands on leadership at all levels.

The next three to four years are likely to be especially demanding, because of the urgent need to address the inequalities of the past, against a background of limited economic growth. Starting towards the middle of this decade, however, I expect more positive factors to come into play, provided the political problems are resolved.

The debt standstill and the difficulties associated with it will be things of the past. South Africa will again enjoy ready access to foreign money and capital markets.

Our existing infrastructure is, by African standards, superb. If there is a reduction in general violence and greater peace in the workplace, we shall be well placed to assume our place at the centre of the sub-continent's economy.

Within this region, socialism is being abandoned and more realistic market-orientated policies are being adopted. This augers well for the future.

Although it may be over-optimistic to expect much new foreign investment, the heavy indirect costs of sanctions to the South African economy will no longer apply.

This country's well-developed transport infrastructure can be utilised better as regional trade improves — particularly in manufacturing — and as tourism increases. Such factors, coupled with the thrust that could come from a more efficiently directed economy and broader patterns of domestic growth, could in turn lead to higher levels of fixed investment and more vigorous expansion in South Africa.

The quest to realise South Africa's undoubted potential will put a high premium on the skill with which we steer the country through the transition phase. As businessmen, we must all be prepared to assume our share of the burden and to take a leading role in the process. No individual or organisation can avoid responsibility for the process of change. At least we can encourage tolerance towards others in our areas of personal influence.

Our society cannot prosper if intolerance prevails.

Chapter Two
A GLOBAL PERSPECTIVE

TONY MANNING

Tony Manning is an independent consultant in
strategic management, corporate communication,
and change. He was formerly Chairman and Chief
Executive Officer of McCann-Erickson advertising
agency, and Marketing Director of Coca-Cola.
He's the author of *Communicating For Change*
(1987), *The New Age Strategist* (1988), and *World
Class!* (1989). His articles appear frequently in
leading business publications, and he runs
seminars and workshops for leading companies.

A s South Africans, we are privileged to live in the most remarkable time. We are caught up in local events we wouldn't have dreamed of a year or two ago. We're also part of a *global* renaissance.

It's essential, as we craft the new South Africa, that we look beyond our own problems and possibilities, and see them in larger context. For as fashionable as it has become to talk of dealing with factors "on the ground" — in townships or on the factory floor, for example — it's equally important to put them in perspective. After 40 years in the wilderness, we're about to rejoin the community of nations. That's good news; but it brings many new challenges for which we're not prepared.

Unintended consequences

In the late 1980s, chaos theory became a hot topic. Scientists, journalists, and businessmen saw in it reasons why "the best laid schemes o' mice an' men gang aft agley" — and why order is often created spontaneously and for no apparent reason.

One phenomenon that intrigues these observers is the so-called "butterfly effect" — the notion that a butterfly can flap its wings in the Amazon forest today and cause a typhoon over Tokyo a month hence. They soon named it "sensitive dependence on initial conditions."

As James Gleick points out in his book *Chaos*, the idea has been around for years:

"For want of a nail, the shoe was lost;
For want of a shoe, the horse was lost;
For want of a horse, the rider was lost;
For want of a rider, the battle was lost;
For want of a battle, the kingdom was lost!"[2]

Any time of change is characterised by uncertainty. With the best will in the world, planners will be wrong. Politicians' decisions won't work out as expected. Businessmen will make mistakes. Our personal plans will often fail.

Surprise, surprise — that's the name of the game of life.

2   James Gleick, *Chaos*, Viking, 1987

That said, we should not underestimate our ability to shape the course of events. The choices we make today will be felt sometime in the future. The results are our responsibility. Expediency will tempt politicians to trade thoughtless insults, to make rash promises, to imply that they can work miracles. But this moment in our history calls for restraint. The angry youth — the so-called "forgotten generation" — will not easily forgive those who let them down.

Short-term gains are always attractive. But choices must be weighed carefully, lest they trigger a future we really don't want.

The age of anxiety

The Japanese are buying America, and many of the most famous western artworks are winding up in Tokyo. Coca-Cola is the universal soft drink. People everywhere wear Levi jeans, Ray Bans, and Giorgio Armani suits; they listen to music on a Sony Walkman — or a Discman if they're into CD's; they drive on Michelin tyres; and they pay for all that with an American Express card.

This is the age of the global citizen; of the global shopper; of the global business. It's an exciting, pulsating time; a time to experiment — and a time to turn back to old-fashioned values.

Back in the 1960s, a Canadian communications expert and philosopher named Marshall McLuhan noted that the world was becoming a "global village." Technology — jet aircraft, television, satellites, inter-continental telecommunications — was linking the farthest corners of the planet. A complex web of communications was re-shaping society.

"This is the Age of Anxiety," said McLuhan, because of "the electric implosion that compels commitment and participation, quite regardless of any 'point of view.' "[3] And he went on to

3   Marshall McLuhan, *Understanding Media: The Extensions Of Man,*
    Routledge and Kegan Paul Ltd, 1964

warn that, as a consequence, "there are no longer any passengers on Spaceship Earth; everybody is crew."

Into the Third Wave

In his best-selling book, *The Third Wave*, Alvin Toffler showed how mankind has advanced through three great "waves of change." First, there was the agricultural wave, which began about 10 000 years ago when man began to till the soil and herd animals for a living. Man's physical strength — augmented by that of animals — was the key resource.

The Industrial Revolution followed in about 1750. Coal and steam power became the transforming resource. Factories churned out mass-produced goods. Great industries were created. Steam trains and steam ships facilitated the transport of passengers and goods. The world started to shrink. Work became specialised, repetitive, cooperative. Management became essential to organise effort. People learned to relate to each other in new ways. Society was restructured, and new roles, rules, and relationships were developed.

The Third Wave — the information age — began around 1955. Then, for the first time, service workers outnumbered production workers in America, computers started to proliferate, and information became the transforming resource.

All three "waves of change" are evident in South Africa. Rural populations still employ the most primitive farming methods. The industrial sector — mining, manufacturing, construction — is still soundly based in the "Second Wave" of change. And a small but growing number of people are involved in "knowledge work."

In most advanced countries, the relative numbers of people involved in each of these three sectors have changed very dramatically. On the one hand, technology — including methods, equipment, fertilizers, herbicides, and pesticides — has made it possible for fewer and fewer farmers to provide the food that society needs. On the other hand, the production of goods and services accounts for a growing chunk of most countries' income — and information is a growing component in that production process.

What does this mean for South Africa?

There is certain to be a tough debate about the redistribution of land; many blacks will want to return to their roots, to own cattle, and to grow crops. This is a highly emotive issue and one which a future government will have to handle with great care.

But while peasant farming might well soak up some unemployment, we should recognise a reality: South Africa is too far down the development path to turn backwards; the aspirations of most South Africans will only be satisfied by a determined move towards Third Wave status, not backwards, into the First Wave.

Land must be equitably available. People who want to live in rural areas, who want to farm, should have that choice. However, over the past two decades, millions of people have moved to urban areas. The future of this country lies in the towns and cities, not on farms.

One of South Africa's strengths in the past has been its ability to produce food. This advantage should be maintained, and the output of our agricultural land must be increased. But the way to do that is through technology — not through massive resettlement of otherwise unemployable people. In other words, new advantages must be built.

The new driving forces of change

Economics and technology are transforming everything we do, and the way we do everything. Sooner or later, their effects will be felt everywhere.

If we ignore the new realities we'll be left behind forever. There just are no odds in playing catch-up when the nature of change itself is changing, and the pace of change is accelerating.

We cannot isolate ourselves and hope to maintain any semblance of our first world standards. Nor will we afford the huge costs which lie ahead as we redress the imbalances brought about by apartheid, and as we strive to create new jobs, build new houses and hospitals and schools, and educate our young people. The "have-nots" in our society will become worse off if we try to go it alone.

Isolation and economic success are mutually exclusive ideals. Unfortunately, too few people understand this.

At precisely the moment when State President De Klerk is opening doors internationally, Mr Mandela and others renew their calls for sanctions. Worse, black opposition groups talk about a new economic order which will, at best, ensure that foreign financiers and businessmen become more and more disinterested in dealing with South Africa.

South Africa, they argue, can become the model non-racial democracy. The new "mixed economy" that they plan will prove that communist and socialist ideas do have merit. The fact that these systems have failed elsewhere is the fault of the people in charge, not of the "ism."

The evidence does not support the argument. And in any event, while politicians' minds are occupied with emotive social matters, the equally vital need for technological progress is largely overlooked.

Without real economic growth, South Africa will not make technological progress. Without real advances in high-tech areas, the economy will sputter along. The two factors are in lock-step. Technology requires two key resources: money and minds. Both are in desperately short supply in South Africa. We simply cannot afford the colossal sums needed to compete in many fields, nor do we have the skills.

To say that South Africa can become a model for other developing countries is an admirable goal. But making it happen won't be easy.

We're late into the game of global competition. The economy is in bad shape. Our markets demand more low-tech than high-tech products.

South Africa's leaders face a tough time. Even while negotiations keep them busy, they must deal with a host of troublesome issues: violence, boycotts, stayaways, marches. The temptation will always be there to focus on the here-and-now, on short-term concerns, and on local issues.

But if this country is to avoid becoming another African basket case, we must look outwards. We must raise our sights, open our doors — and become global players.

The living room war

It wasn't too long ago that the only people who saw a football match or a beauty pageant were the lucky ones who could get there. Now, courtesy of television, thousands of millions of people around the world are real-time spectators at Wimbledon, the World Cup, and the Olympic Games.

When pop star Madonna appears live in a concert in Rome, there we are, too. During a special remembrance service for former Beatles star John Lennon, his song "Imagine" is broadcast from United Nations headquarters in New York to an audience of *one billion* people all over the world — to one in five human beings on the planet. Other pop stars — singing in English — raise untold amounts of money for starving children and for the protection of Amazon forests.

Events like these tell us something is happening which changes forever the way we see things, the way we can deal with things, and the way we have to think about things. And it changes forever the way that we might function as individuals in this country, our perceptions of one another, and our political possibilities.

TV is a great entertainment medium. It has also become a potent political weapon. By making information instantly and widely available, it has transformed war, as it has transformed every other social activity.

In the good old days, wars were fought on the battlefield with bullets and bombs. News of their progress took days, weeks — perhaps even months or years — to reach home. The information that trickled back from the battle lines was censored; that way, the folks at home wouldn't know how bad things really were and the enemy would gain little by way of intelligence.

Today, however, investigative journalism and technology combine to bring wars to the world's living rooms. The Middle East crisis has become a real-time soap opera with an audience of millions, perhaps billions. Politicians understand this. They cultivate their TV "presence." Their media advisers carefully manage photo opportunities, and they talk in "sound bites" that TV audiences easily understand.

Shortly after Iraq invaded Kuwait, US President George Bush took a holiday. He also took care to be seen relaxing on his fishing boat or a golf cart. No sign of panic; this was a tough man in total charge!

Coverage by CNN and other major TV networks takes us into the desert at all hours of the day and night. Retired politicians posture as statesmen and rescuers, and fly to Iraq on mercy missions. Saddam Hussein stages bizarre appearances with his terrified hostages. Prominent newscasters visit Baghdad to talk to the man widely regarded as another Hitler. A Saddam look-alike appears regularly to give the Iraqi leader's view.

President Bush tries to sell his tough stance back home; the polls show that voters are getting tired of the whole process, and are less and less keen on war. Radio and TV talk shows, magazines and newspapers examine the crisis from all angles: the cost, the possibility of war, and the consequences.

Here, for the first time, is a war which involves not just the protagonists, or a small group of politicians, but every one of us. A war fought not just in government buildings, statesmen's offices, or even the UN, but in lounges and living rooms, in mansions and in mud huts absolutely everywhere.

Suddenly, every one of us is a crew member, every one of us bears some responsibility for the future of this world of ours. None of us can escape the changes that are will happen as a result of events in the Middle East — as seen in living colour on TV.

Why communism really failed

Communism has failed, and its staunchest advocates are trying desperately to introduce capitalist concepts. Socialism is being buried everywhere, and even the looniest leftists are flailing around for some new ideology to grab onto. The infamous Berlin Wall has been breached, and bits of it are being sold as souvenirs. There's a McDonald's hamburger joint on Red Square. The Soviet Union is flying apart as Mr Gorbachev's notions of *glasnost* and *perestroika* take hold. Emissaries from Czechoslovakia, Poland, and Rumania visit Pretoria.

What has caused these momentous events? Why has communism failed? Why has socialism been discredited? What made Gorbachev make a U-turn (after all, wasn't he a dyed-in-the-wool communist, a loyal Party man?)

One might advance many complex reasons for these remarkable changes. But at heart, just two matter: the Soviet economy ran out of steam, and Soviet technology was hopelessly outmoded.

As we entered the 1980s, the Soviet Union posed a serious military threat to the world. By most estimates, it was a great deal more powerful — in terms of both weapons and men — than the US.

But then US President Ronald Reagan countered with America's two great strengths: economic power and technology. He escalated the arms race, pouring billions of dollars into it and giving the nod to the high-tech "Star Wars" programme.

As the key player in the world economy — a nation of outwardly-focused, export-oriented, wealth-driven entrepreneurs — the US had resources to spare. The Soviets, on the other hand, could barely afford their daily bread. They were economically and technologically bankrupt; the bureaucrats were helpless; their ideology was useless. In short, they just couldn't keep up.

Once this became apparent, the Soviet Union's restless client states quickly pressed for independence from Moscow. Unable to afford to support their dictators, Gorbachev let go. The game was over in a matter of months.

The failure of communism and totalitarianism offers a singularly important lesson to South Africa's future leaders. The Soviet Union and Eastern Europe face daunting challenges as they try to re-invent themselves and reintegrate themselves into the world economy. Their chances of success are not good. South Africa will have an equally tough time of it. Playing catch-up in the new competitive arena is not easy. Without help from already successful players — through direct or indirect investment, loans, technology transfers, or strategic alliances — it's impossible.

Trapped in time

As we closed out the 1980s, economics and technology forced a worldwide reassessment of how things work. A young American political scientist named Frances Fukuyama proclaimed, in a controversial essay, that we'd come to "the end of history."[4]

But he was wrong. All we've come to is a new starting point — what *Fortune* magazine called "The Era of Possibilities."[5]

Strangely, however, South Africa seems caught in a timewarp. For at the very moment when communists and socialists are adopting "evil" capitalist ideas, black organisations like the ANC and the PAC talk of nationalisation, redistribution — and even more government interference than we already have. And the South African Communist Party embarks on a recruiting drive.

At the very time when the National Party is seeing the light, and turning its back on crazy concepts that have brought this country to the very brink of disaster, black politicians and their advisers are seriously considering even more of the same.

If nothing else convinces them that this is a foolish course, this country's socialist past should be proof enough. National Party rule has been characterised by social engineering,

4 Frances Fukuyama, "The End Of History?" *The National Interest*, Summer 1989
5 "The Era Of Possibilities," *Fortune* cover story, January 15, 1990

toadyism, favouritism, control, bureaucracy — and big government. The result has been dreadful inequality; desperate living conditions for millions of people; soaring unemployment; poverty, crime, and disease; a hopeless education system; and high inflation and taxation, together with falling productivity and low economic growth.

Is this litany of failure really to become the roadmap for our future?

Logic bubbles

The information age requires new behaviours, new attitudes, and new skills. And perhaps the most vital skill of all is that of creatively coping with change.

Most of us resist change because we are trapped in what Edward de Bono calls a "logic bubble." We have a certain set of perceptions, a certain set of "mental junk" that we've carted around from childhood. We started gathering it when we were very young — sights, sounds, touch, tastes, smells, things people said to us, experiences and so on. We gathered it onto our mental "tape recording" and we now use it to see the world, to make judgments, and to think.

As a result, we don't think as creatively as we might. We don't listen readily to new ideas. We don't adapt easily to change. We like the stuff that we hold in our heads, and we don't readily let old ideas out or new ideas in. So, as Oscar Wilde once said, "Most of us think we're thinking when all we're doing is rearranging our prejudices."

Our logic bubbles don't only hamper our ability to think. They also hamper our communication.

When we talk to each other from our private worlds — from our positions of prejudice — we often talk past each other. We distort each other's messages. We jump to conclusions about how the other sees things, wants things, or feels.

As we move towards the 21st Century, we're going to have to learn to poke holes in our logic bubbles, to let some of our old ideas out and to risk hearing some new ones. We're going to have to learn to walk in each other's logic bubbles, to see other people's perspectives, and to understand what is going on in other people's minds.

As change explodes around us, we must give more attention to issues "out there" in the global village — politics, economics, demographics, technology, and so on. But in the process of creating a new society, we must not lose sight of ourselves. For that is where the most significant changes are taking place. Man is different from other animals in that we have the power to deliberately change ourselves and our environment. Yet it is not in our nature to deal well with change. When it occurs, we react in predictable fashion: fear, resistance, acceptance, adaptation, and exhaustion. Too often, we waste too much energy on fear and resistance, and too little on managing our transformation. The result is perhaps a less satisfying future than we might wish for. Little wonder, then, that most of us are over-stressed, wrung out — exhausted by it all.

Similar values

Time and again, when I ask mixed groups what they want in the "new South Africa," they list the same five things: peace, opportunities, education, security, and love.

Agreeing on these objectives is a good starting point. This is a religious country, and there is a huge reservoir of goodwill among the masses.

Some people suggest that the key to our future lies in blending the best aspects of all of our cultures. They talk of the "South Africanisation of business," and point to the African concept of *ubuntu* — community — as an example of what is possible.

There might be some merit in this idea, but we should not forget the realities of life in the global village. There might be new concern for the environment, a growing interest in art, and greater concern about family life and social investment, but this is not yet the "kinder, gentler world" that George Bush wanted. It's one tough neighbourhood.

The only standard of performance that counts is "world class." So every effort must be made to raise people's abilities to the highest level, rather than lower our sights and accept mediocrity.

The idea of community might help us realise this goal. For it implies more than spiritual accord or widely-held values; it has, too, a practical side which psychologist M. Scott Peck describes so well:

> "Because a community includes members with many different points of view and the freedom to express them, it comes to appreciate the whole of a situation far better than an individual, couple, or ordinary group can. Incorporating the dark and the light, the sacred and the profane, the sorrow and the joy, the glory and the mud, its conclusions are well rounded. Nothing is likely to be left out. With so many frames of reference, it approaches reality more and more closely. Realistic decisions, consequently, are more often guaranteed in community than in any other human environment."[6]

The institutions of the past are obsolete. We have the opportunity now to re-design our country, from the top down and the bottom up.

The starting point is to recognise the astonishing changes that are transforming the world, and to accept that the future will not — and cannot — be a replay of the past. What lies ahead will be more surprising than anything that occurred in the past. We will have to invent totally new responses if we are to survive.

In search of options

Psychologists tell us that as we mature, we expand both the range of our options and our repertoire of responses. Several well-known theories describe this growth in different ways. For example, Abraham Maslow talked of a "hierarchy of needs" — physiological, safety, social, esteem, self-actualisation. Professor Clare Graves said that people could be slotted into seven categories (reactive — tribalistic — egocentric — conformist

6 M. Scott Peck, *The Different Drum*, Rider & Co., 1987

— manipulative — socio-centric — existential) according to
their values and lifestyles. And according to Professor Chris
Argyris of Harvard University, the path looks like this:

PASSIVE INFANT → ACTIVE ADULT
DEPENDENT → INDEPENDENT
FEW BEHAVIOURS → MANY BEHAVIOURS
CASUAL RELATIONSHIPS → COMMITMENT
SHORT-TERM → LONG-TERM
SUBORDINATE → EQUAL OR SUPERIOR
UNAWARE → AWARE

In this country, unfortunately, we have a vast number of adults
who make life and death decisions about their own lives virtually every day — yet they've been treated like children.

This presents a real problem. South Africa is now burdened
with millions of dependent people who don't know how to assert
themselves. At the same time, they're being rapidly exposed to
a whole new set of possibilities, to a new world — a new global
neighbourhood.

The images of this global neighbourhood, the experiences it
offers, and the pressures it presents will all force people to move
very rapidly up the path towards maturity. As they grow, these
people will want more out of life, they'll expect more, and
they'll demand more. So while we might have a serious crisis of
expectations already, it's almost sure to get worse.

Political, business, and trade union leaders will have to learn
to respond appropriately. Behaviour that's OK at the top today
simply won't be tolerated by people who understand their options and are prepared to stand up for their rights.

The new global citizen will exhibit a number of characteristics which for most of us are totally foreign. We'll have to
learn to deal with them in new ways.

1. **Information junkie.** A key characteristic of the global
   neighbourhood is that it is "information-rich." People are
   exposed to a wide variety of information all the time —
   newspapers, magazines, television, and so on. They're well
   informed about their choices.

2. **Short attention span.** The new global citizen is a very fickle person. There's so much "noise"in the environment, so many attractions and distractions, that we can change our minds and make new choices at a moment's notice.

3. **Experimenter — but also brand loyal.** The new global citizen likes new experiences — but also wants some guarantees. In this world of uncertainty, surprise, and rapid change, we seek some form of stability. Brands go some way to providing it. Their power in this new world is absolutely enormous. Companies everywhere will have to pour more time and attention into building their brands. (Companies that try to export goods will be at a very serious disadvantage in this regard, because they won't be able to afford the huge investment that brand-building takes in overseas markets.)

4. **Return to old-fashioned values.** Even while we experiment and learn to push out our limits, old-fashioned values are making a comeback. Religious organisations report growing interest. Art sales are soaring. Museums are an extremely acceptable form of alternative entertainment. Theatre and ballet draw big crowds. AIDS is transforming sexual behaviour.

The leadership constraint

On February 2, 1990, State President FW de Klerk turned our world upside down. What made him change? Why did he suddenly see the light? Here, after all, is a man who was regarded as one of the more conservative members of PW Botha's cabinet.

There are certainly many deeply personal reasons. De Klerk is a religious man and might well have felt that the policies of his party stood on shaky moral, ethical, or religious ground. But such reasons would only accelerate an inevitable process. Simply put, De Klerk had no choice. He is a prisoner of his context.

Like Gorbachev, De Klerk has no option but to bring about serious reforms. (The big question: which of the two men is more likely to succeed?)

Five years ago, then State President PW Botha could act in a certain way and get away it. De Klerk has less room for manoeuvre. For whereas Botha saw his canvas as essentially South African, De Klerk has stretched his vision to embrace not just Southern Africa, but indeed, many other countries much further afield. Also, world pressure on South Africa has become intolerable. We might not like the idea of foreigners "interfering in our affairs," but we do have to pay attention.

What this means, of course, is that the move away from apartheid really is irreversible. The clock cannot be turned back. Politicians who say that external pressure on the South African government must be maintained, that we must wait for meaningful signs that apartheid is forever dead, are in dreamland. Apartheid *is* dead. The process of transforming this society is clearly under way, and there is no turning back now.

Hopefully, as this becomes clear, tomorrow's leaders will not be tempted by delusions of omnipotence. Hopefully, they will grasp the fact that they cannot act in splendid isolation.

We can't ignore the new realities

Before 1950 it was possible for national governments to act independently. Since then, however, it has become increasingly difficult. Isolation has two effects: firstly, it encourages creative thinking, as some people set out to beat the system; secondly, it saps a country's resources. And the most important resource to first be stretched and then sapped, is entrepreneurial thought.

For some time yet, black opposition leaders will try to control South Africa's links with the world. They will try to manage the pace of change in all spheres — politics, economics, sport, culture, or whatever — until they decide that the process of reform is "irreversible."

White right-wing groups will interfere with our global connections in a different way. By clinging to the past, and through random acts of anti-black violence, they'll do their bit to slow down the negotiating process, and to scare off foreign politicians, investors, and tourists. There's little doubt in their view that reform is reversible — and must be reversed. Both the left and the right are ignoring the new realities.

Just as economics and technology have transformed the world, so have they also changed this country, its possibilities, and its path to the future. Once South Africa was a proud and respected member of the League of Nations. But since 1948 we have become progressively more distanced: apartheid has made us an outcast, a pariah, an undesirable. And since 1985, when major foreign banks shut off their funding, when key foreign countries began to impose sanctions, and when disinvestment began in earnest, this country has been out on a limb.

Now, we're on the comeback trail. State President FW de Klerk has declared the moves away from apartheid "irreversible." He and his diplomats are being welcomed in the capitals of the world. South African businessmen are finding doors opening to them. Countries such as Madagascar and the Soviet Union are encouraging South African tourists. Soon, we may be allowed to visit Egypt.

As the new South Africa takes shape, there can be no passengers; everybody must be "crew." We are all neighbours, and we have a joint responsibility to each other, to our country — and to our planet.

As we become global citizens, we face new challenges and new opportunities. We no longer act in isolation. Our personal lives, our business organisations, and our social institutions will all be transformed by this fact.

The process of change hinges on many factors. Most important of all, it hinges on economic growth, for if we do not "bake a bigger cake," we simply won't be able to fund the future. It is time for South Africa to become a world class competitor.

Converging standards

Today, in market after market, standards are converging. Differences in productivity, quality, price, and performance are being ironed out. People everywhere are exposed to the same products and services, and to brand names and promotional messages that sell a universal "good life."

"One sight, one sound, one sell" is the new formula behind many marketing campaigns. Customers respond by buying the same things, doing the same things, and enjoying the same pleasures. Once again, economics and technology are driving the changes.

Some South Africa marketing experts argue that race and culture are of little importance when it comes to buying behaviour; buying *power* is what counts. So, they say, it makes sense to think in terms of "marketing bands" — the steps on the economic ladder — that really make the difference.

There's some truth in this view. As social, political, and legal barriers fall away, blacks are entering the mainstream economy with a vengeance. They're big spenders in casinos in the TBVC states, and at the Turffontein race course. They're starting to check into five-star hotels for weekend breaks. Shops like Woolworths, Pick 'n Pay, and Edgars have a rapidly growing black clientele. And really up-market luxury stores like Levisons, Derbers, and A&D Spitz all depend largely on blacks to buy their exclusive imported goods.

It's hard, by glancing at the pages of *Style* (a "white" magazine) and *Tribute* (a "black" magazine), to tell which magazine is which.

Both publications give a lot of space to photos of the "in" set at play. And what do we see? People of all colours having the same kind of fun (in fact, aren't they *the same people* in both magazines?)

The fashion pages in both *Style* and *Tribute* look identical — gorgeous models, gorgeous clothes. The food pages could easily be run in either magazine without changing anything. A spread on up-and-comers in *Tribute* would not be out of place in *Style* (any white would surely be proud to achieve what these young blacks have achieved!) And no doubt many of the articles in *Style* would appeal to *Tribute's* audience.

TV4 (a "white" station) today has more black viewers than whites. The Bill Cosby show is a favourite with conservative

Afrikaners, while Dallas and Dynasty have huge black audiences. An increasing number of advertisers include people of various races in their "crossover" TV commercials — and the language is English. It's tempting to agree, on the basis of this evidence, that we're all the same under our skin. But as we shall see, that's too glib a judgement.

As far back as the 1960s, Marshall McLuhan, Peter Drucker, and a number of others had predicted that the world was becoming a single economic entity. But it wasn't until 1983, when Theodore Levitt wrote his landmark *Harvard Business Review* article on "The Globalization of Markets," that anyone paid much attention. Then, the real implications hit home.

Levitt, a professor of marketing at the Harvard Business School, went beyond yet another forecast; he reported the facts as they were unfolding:

"Suddenly no place and nobody is insulated from the alluring attractions of modernity. Almost everybody everywhere wants all the things they have heard about, seen, or experienced via the new technological facilitators that drive their wants and wishes. And it drives these increasingly into global community, thus homogenising markets everywhere."[7]

What this meant, of course, was that economies of scale were essential. Companies had to become "world class" — in size, in competence, in the boldness of their vision.

This emphasis on bigness for survival's sake has forced companies to re-examine their priorities and the way they do business. Coupled with the new economic and technological realities, it has triggered strategies which would have been unthinkable only a few years ago.

Shopping for value

Whereas yesterday's conventional wisdom was that every function in the value chain should be performed as close to home as

7 Theodore Levitt, "The Globalization of Markets," *Harvard Business Review*, May/June 1983

possible, now companies buy what they need from wherever in
the world it makes most sense. So R&D happens in one city,
design in another; components are manufactured in one country,
and assembled halfway around the world.

This had led to the phenomenon of the "hollow" or the
"stateless" corporation. It has also led to a concept known as
"bodyshopping" — the purchase of labour from wherever in the
world it's cheapest or most skilled.

Ted Levitt's article was incredibly influential in the world of
business. Any number of major companies spent untold millions
— if not billions — of dollars, pounds, marks, yen, or whatever,
trying to "go global." Most failed.

For even as economics and technology have created a global
marketplace, so they have given customers virtually infinite
choices. Management has been forced to learn "micro-market-
ing."

Coca-Cola is one of the very few brand names that appeals
to people of all ages, in every country. But one reason for Coke's
enormous success in recent years has been its so-called "mega-
brand strategy" which gives consumers a range of products
under the Coca-Cola banner — including Coke, Coke Classic,
or Cherry Coke, plus diet or caffeine-free options of each.

Sony launches a new product every 1,5 days. Seiko designs
a new watch every day. An increasing number of firms now
shower the market with new, different, and better products and
services — launched at astonishing speed.

Levitt was right when he said that global markets were a
reality. But while individuals will go out of their way to find the
brand that satisfies them best, they also search for identity; so
they want tailored products and services under the safety of that
brand umbrella.

Competing in the new arena

Ten years ago, Professor Michael Porter of the Harvard Business
School said that there were basically two ways to compete. A
firm could either be the low-cost producer or the differentiator.

In addition, management had to choose whether to aim at the mass market or at a niche. The most dangerous place to be, said Porter, was "stuck in the middle."

In the past decade, however, we've seen a growing number of aggressive companies challenge these views. They now drive down their costs and add value at the same time. And while they might want to grab as much of the mass market as possible, they're slicing it up into smaller and smaller segments. "Micromarketing" is the new reality.

Everything I've said so far has huge implications for the way firms will be managed in the future. They'll naturally have to become intensely customer-focused — as opposed to just customer-*aware*. They'll have to manage their people in totally new ways. And above all, they'll have to pay far more attention to building their "invisible assets" — knowledge, skills, attitude, brands, patents, the corporate image, customer loyalty, etc. These are all "soft" issues, and hard to measure. Right now, they're not nearly as important in most companies as the "hard" issues, the visible assets — plant, equipment, buildings, vehicles, cash — which appear on the balance sheet. But they're the factors that will make the difference between success and failure a new global society.

The choice is ours

The changes that are happening affect all of us. We are all crew members on this spaceship, "new South Africa." We've just set off on a wonderfully exciting journey. We don't know the destination, and the ride is sure to be bumpy, frightening, and dangerous.

None of us can ignore the challenges. None of us can sit back and be a passenger. None of us will be unchanged by the experience.

The future is what we make it.

Chapter Three
POLITICAL CHANGE: THE OVER-ARCHING ISSUE

WYNAND MALAN

Wynand Malan practised as an attorney in
Johannesburg for many years before he was elected
National Party MP for Randburg in 1977. Ten
years later he resigned from the Party but kept his
seat as an independent candidate. He was a
co-founder of the National Democratic Movement,
and, in 1989, of the Democratic Party. He resigned
as co-leader in July 1990, saying, "That for which I
have worked has become reality. The process is
moving inevitably towards a negotiated
settlement." He has resumed a full-time legal
career in Randburg.

If everything goes well, these are likely to be the key elements of a political scenario in South Africa:

1. We will have a negotiated constitution within two to four years. This constitution will include:
   — A justiciable bill of rights
   — Federal elements with checks and balances
   — Guarantees of multi-party politics
   — Guarantees of limited segmental autonomy.
2. A new government will be in place. It will be:
   — A black government
   — An ANC-led government.
3. Whites will have vacated the centre of power politics and we will see:
   — The NP culture leading an accommodated opposition in Parliament
   — Whites, and particularly Afrikaners, very active on the periphery of politics in segmental autonomous areas of cultural interests, including — and mainly — education.
   — The PAC, AZAPO, and Inkatha will act as counter-balancing forces. They will not be democratic, and they will be minority organisations, but they'll secure the working of multi-party democracy. The PAC and AZAPO will function on a national level, while Inkatha will function more especially on a regional level.
   — Organised business bargaining directly with Government about policies that affect its interests.
   — Organised labour representing the interests of employed people, becoming more of an ally of business, with Government representing the unemployed.

Leadership differences

The commitment of the ANC leadership and the National Party government to a political settlement, and acceptance of their joint sponsorship of the process leading to settlement, should not be underestimated. It is total. To this extent the process is indeed irreversible. There is no turning back.

The relationship is good and mutual trust exists. At the same time, both are not too sure of the other's ability to bring their constituencies along.

The leadership culture in the NP government is very different to that within the ANC. A failure to discount this difference could lead to an incorrect reading of developments.

Within the NP the culture of representative government is fully established. De Klerk will be followed regardless, because he is the leader. This explains the zeal with which the party follows him on policies that a year ago were anathema to their thinking.

The ANC, on the other hand, has a culture of participative decision making. It is a liberation movement, a quasi-nationalistic movement, and will remain so for some time after it has formally transformed itself into a political party.

The rapid pace of events since February 2, 1990 put tremendous strain on Mandela in particular and the ANC leadership in general. Opportunity for the traditional networking was virtually non-existent. Considering that ANC leaders have often had to respond instantaneously, and have had to follow their political gut, they have generally not done too badly.

The December congress (in doubt when this book went to press) is a key development for the establishment of structures for more effective networking of future decisions.

Furthermore, ANC leadership is symbolic of the liberation struggle. The December congress will procure an integration of prison, exile, and internal leadership. Individuals will fall by the wayside when office bearers are elected. But they will remain loyal and active within the organisation, and will not lose their influence.

A power struggle or a split in the liberation movement is a myth. The shared commitment to the goal of liberation, the spirit of "nationalism," over-rides whatever internal differences may exist. The new integrated leadership will herald the fomenting of a front, not the excommunication of individuals.

Bring on the clowns

The violence we are experiencing is natural — even "healthy." There are many facets to the phenomenon of violence. Without referring to all of them, to my mind the fundamental issue lies in the simultaneous existence of a host of different value systems which in their nature are not able to cope politically with each other in the absence of a legitimate coordinating authority.

The animistic, hierarchically structured, traditional society with its hereditary leadership does not tolerate any concept of western type democracy which by definition is threatening of its culture and stability.

The "one right way" of the more absolutistic "true believers" of certain liberation ideologies again by definition does not tolerate alternative options.

And "best alternative" thinking is crowded out by any of the other value systems.

On top of all this, only a threat to the dominant value system or "mind-set" of a person causes him to shift to some other mind-set or value system. During this shift he becomes, because of his insecurity, extremely assertive, and often acts like an emperor.

Another dimension, which may seem minor at present, but which can have disastrous effects if not addressed early, is the perception of some in the constituencies of both Government and the ANC that negotiation is a sham agenda and that the real agenda still lives at leadership level within the "holy war" of struggle versus system.

To address this reality, the symbols of Magnus Malan and Chris Hani will soon be actively involved in negotiations, to shatter perceptions of hidden (original) agendas.

White right wing violence, much feared in certain circles, is not as real as believed. Leadership of the right wing is still responsible, and will remain so by any standards.

Violence during the transition can and will be managed. Incidents of violence during the process to settlement will be very much like clowns in a good circus. To move from the lion and tiger to the trapeze necessitates a change of scenery. While that happens, clowns will entertain the audience. They'll amuse some children and scare others. But the trapeze will end the perfect show.

Joint responsibility

The key concept for and during the process will be "joint responsibility."

Both Government and the ANC are intellectually committed to the process of transition to a democratic constitution. Yet as to the result, they are both still emotionally lacking. Government still speaks as if it will carry the burden of authority for the next decade and more. The ANC fails to accept responsibility for anything but political success.

The idea of interim government surfaces regularly but without content. No one has any idea how it can be implemented. This can be understood. There are no democratic structures under the constitution in which the ANC can share authority and thus responsibility. These will have to develop informally and almost organically.

Participation by the ANC in executive decision making without the necessary institutional authority may make the leaders of that movement look like sell-outs to their followers if the results aren't acceptable.

The government finds itself in a similar position. Sharing office officially without its constituency perceiving positive results — mainly stability — will put tremendous pressure on Government.

Both parties are aware of the need to manage the process in such a way that it broadens to multi-party participation. The relevant actors are the PAC, AZAPO, and the CP.

The latter is divided between those who want to participate in the negotiations more or less on the Carel Boshoff line:

negotiating a "Volkstaat" as part of a package deal, accepting black rule as a result of a democratic constitution. On the other hand, there are those who actually accept the same but stay in the protest politics mode.

Both the PAC and AZAPO are ready to participate. In fact, they demand elections for a negotiating forum, rejecting negotiation but favouring peaceful settlement. Their rhetoric will remain confusing within the liberation vocabulary, but there's no doubt that their leadership, too, is responsible.

All other parties are already, in one way or another, part of the process.

Therefore, while managing their respective images, the NP government and the ANC will establish an "interim government" through joint and *ad hoc* structures in various areas of policy making, including both crisis management and long-term planning in such areas as Education, Law and Order, and Health and Housing. Through these "interim government structures" inputs into the budget — or, rather, decisions on it — will be made.

Some form of consensus on a future order will develop before real negotiations commence.

The value of a constituent assembly

As part of its game plan, the ANC envisages the election of a negotiating forum.

Government, on the other hand, rejects the concept, arguing for a multi-party negotiating process in which all leaders with a "proven constituency" will participate. How this will be decided isn't clear; the matter is likely to be informally negotiated.

However, there's no doubt that some key players in government are already considering the possibility that — in due time and after some informal and multi-party, yet not all-inclusive, negotiations — there could be a move to the election on a proportional representative system of a formal negotiating body

to decide on a future constitution. This would have very obvious
advantages:

1. It would determine the relative weight of the players, margi-
   nalising smaller, more extremist, groupings.
2. It would provide a constitutional and democratic transition.
3. It might obviate the need for a referendum or elections under
   the present constitution, as all parties would probably get
   involved — or relinquish their claim to legitimacy.

It is unlikely that the elected negotiating forum would transform
itself into a first parliament. Elections would follow in terms of
an agreed constitution, endorsed and ratified by the existing
parliament.

Problems of social management

The return of exiles — some 30 000 people — will bring major
logistical problems. All of them are employed by, or at least in
the care of, the liberation movements. To find some accommo-
dation for them in a "spears to ploughshares" programme, providing some form of social security, and simply providing
aircraft for their return, requires major organisation and cooperation.

South Africa lacks the skills to deal with this problem. The
experience of the international community — through the
United Nations — might usefully be procured.

The private sector could also play a major role in guaran-
teeing apprenticeships or job opportunities.

The economic policy debate

The debate about a future economy is stale. The business community seems unable to come to grips with the reality of a black
government whose priority will be equitable distribution economic politics.

We continue to hear the rhetoric of privatisation versus
nationalisation, of a free market versus control, of socialism
versus capitalism.

Until the business sector accepts that the national goal of a future government will be to enhance the living standards of its power base, primarily through distributive policies which will drastically redetermine budget priorities, and until business becomes actively involved in planning such policies with the future government's planners, it will be unable to positively influence government thinking and policies towards markets and growth.

Future power politics, coalitions, and alliances

Under the "holy war" scenario the NP and the ANC found themselves on the extremes. Since the ascent of De Klerk and Mandela they've become co-sponsors of transition, and have found themselves in the centre of our politics.

The irony is that, after elections, they're likely to find themselves in opposition to one another in a new parliament, albeit accommodating each other in this new relationship. In any normal democratic society, prevailing value systems in their constituencies would have made them political allies.

The culture and nature of liberation and of nationalism doesn't allow common cause with the oppressor while collecting the prize of struggle.

Even if the ANC does not obtain an absolute majority, it's more likely to seek alliances with AZAPO and the PAC than with De Klerk's NP or whichever party he may then belong to. Nor will the political culture of any other black organisation allow it to forge close links with the NP.

The ANC must be the banker in the jackpot of a future South Africa.

Chapter Four

WHERE THE ECONOMY IS HEADED

DR AZAR JAMMINE

Dr Azar Jammine is a director and Chief
Economist of Econometrix (Pty) Ltd, an
independent economic research, analysis, and
consulting company. He is also a director of the
Fedsure group and of Safegro Unit Trust
Management Company. He completed honours
degrees in statistics and economics at the
University of the Witwatersrand while working as
an investment analyst, first for a merchant bank
and then for a firm of Johannesburg stockbrokers.
He completed his Masters degree in economics at
the London School of Economics in 1976, and
obtained his PhD from the London Business
School, paying his way by doing numerous
consulting projects in Europe, America, and the
Far East.

Only a year ago, it would have been very difficult to imagine what the world economy and what the South African economy's prospects would look like today. There have been some amazing changes, both overseas and in South Africa.

Change causes apprehension. In Eastern Europe, people are now faced with inflation, riots, and violence. In South Africa, similarly, we're faced with a very uncertain and fluctuating environment.

However, this time of enormous change also brings exceptional opportunities. And one doesn't need to look very far to see what they might be.

A legacy of inequality

The biggest problem we face is massive inequality in the distribution of income and wealth. It's the highest in the world amongst countries where one can measure it. Bridging the gap between the haves and the have-nots — in areas such as housing, education, health, transport and electricity — offers many possibilities.

To solve the housing problem by the end of the decade, we need to build more than 1 000 houses a day at a cost of around R5 billion per annum. That's equivalent to 7% of our annual budget.

There are presently some seven million people living in squatter camps. Two million squatters live within walking distance of the Durban Parade.

Four out of five households don't have electricity. To solve that problem, and to try and provide electricity to all the households in the country, ESKOM estimates that we need to spend R1,4 billion a year between now and the year 2000.

We're in desperate need of hospitals. The 11 500 unused beds in white areas won't begin to solve the shortage of hospital and general health care. Two million children suffer from malnutrition. The infant mortality rate in Soweto is 80 per 1000, which compares with an average infant mortality amongst whites of 20 per 1000. The cost of AIDS will be devastating.

On the educational front, it's estimated that to arrive at parity between the different groups we need 33 000 new classrooms by the end of the decade. And we need to increase the education budget from its present level of around 19% of the total budget to more like 50% of the total budget.

We need to spend a tremendous amount to improve the transport infrastructure of the country, to bring people closer to their jobs. By one estimate, South Africans on average live three times as far from their place of work as in overseas countries.

Probably the most pressing issue is education. Without proper education and training there is no way this country can really uplift itself. If we did make a concerted effort in this area, we could make significant progress by the turn of the century. But the costs would be mind-boggling.

Can we afford what we must do?

Creating equality of opportunity by the year 2000 would require an increase in the country's present budget of something like 50% a year at current prices. At the moment the government spends roughly R73 billion a year. To solve our housing, educational, and health problems by the turn of the century, we'd need to spend an additional R30 billion to R50 billion each year.

The question is, how do you find that money? Do you leave it to government, or do you pull in the private sector? This is the subject of great debate.

One view has it that when economic sanctions are lifted, everything will come right. I would caution against such optimism, because South Africa's economic growth rate has declined for the last 20 years. Sanctions only really came into place around 1985. Another view is that the informal sector holds the key to our future. Since 1985, the government has effected substantial deregulation, and enormous opportunities have been opened up in the informal sector.

But I don't think one should see the informal sector as the salvation of our economy. The reason it's so large is that unemployment is so high. The population is growing extremely fast.

We need 400 000 new jobs a year just to stop unemployment from getting worse. Things would have been very much worse were it not for the informal sector, and the informal sector itself is driven by the overall economy. Some estimates suggest that the informal sector could account for as much 40% of economic activity. But a study conducted by the Central Statistical Service said it made up no more than 7% of GNP. And my own calculations suggest roughly 12% to 13% of overall economic activity.

The size of this sector is impressive; but more important is its *rate of growth* — about 10% per annum. If we take that into account, then clearly many statistics underestimate the overall real economic growth rate by around 1,2% to 1,3% percent per annum.

Government follies

The simple fact is, there is no quick fix. In spite of the enormous opportunities to spend money and uplift the masses of our people socially, if we carry on as we have for the past 20 years we face disaster. Our living standards will decline immeasurably.

One fundamental reason for our poor economic performance has been the enormous increase in Government's role in overall economic activity since 1971.

To pay for its spending, taxes have been raised dramatically. They've gone up virtually non-stop since 1960, and the rate of increase accelerated after 1980.

Of course, as people have been taxed more and more, so their disposable incomes have declined. The general standard of living is no higher today than it was ten years ago.

In addition, higher taxes have meant that South Africa's productivity has fallen way behind the rest of the world. And it's not just the developed countries which have moved ahead of us; since 1981, many developing countries also passed us.

Disposable income falls

People have tried to compensate for the erosion in their disposal incomes in various ways.

On the one hand, they've reduced their savings; so personal savings as a percentage of disposal income has declined from an average of 10% in the late 1970s to virtually nothing at present. They've also borrowed more. So the 1980s have been characterised by tremendous surges in the demand for credit for all sorts of purchases.

Unfortunately this growth in credit demand has been aided and abetted by the banking system. South Africa has a small number of banks which are all controlled by massive financial institutions. They know that they don't have to be too responsible in their lending habits, because should they over- extend themselves and land in trouble, they'll be bailed out.

The growth in credit demand has caused tremendous surges in the growth in our money supply — and in inflation. The authorities have then been forced to raise interest rates, and a bust has followed. This cycle has been repeated over and over again. Right now we're in the bust phase, in a recession, with negative growth once more.

Needed: more realistic interest rates

While inflation has come down a long way in the rest of the world, South Africa's inflation rate has remained very high since 1980. So we've had higher government expenditure, higher taxation, lower disposable income — and higher inflation as a result.

This process has also been helped by Government's own monetary policy in the past, which kept interest rates artificially low for lengthy periods of time.

The first step in opening up longer term opportunities is to try and keep interest rates at more realistic levels. They should at least be kept in line with overseas economies, when adjusted for inflation.

Pain before gain

With a new regime at the Reserve Bank, and under a new State President, we have for the past year had far more realistic interest rates. I believe that if they're maintained, they'll bring new order to the economy.

However, to keep real interest rates high you first have to go through a sort of "hangover." And that's what we're suffering from right now.

A key question we must ask is: have we got the time for the economic restructuring that's required? Can we, for instance, keep interest rates positive in real terms at all times — especially in the face of the tremendous growth in unemployment? Already there are increasing pressures on the authorities to reduce interest rates to rescue the situation.

The shifting tax burden

The tax structure has contributed enormously to the distortions in the South African economy, and to the decline in our living standards.

A glance at South Africa's tax curve shows how much higher our taxes are than those of other countries overseas. What's more, the rate at which one goes up the tax ladder is enormously steep. And when your taxable income increases in a time of inflation, you move up that curve at an inordinately steep rate. The effect has been to shift the burden of taxation sharply onto the private individual over the past decade. In 1980/81, individual income tax contributed no more than 15% of government revenue. By 1990, that had risen to over 30%. In addition, GST had risen from 12% of government revenue to 26%.

In contrast, the mining sector's share of taxation fell from 27% to virtually nothing at all.

The changing pattern of savings

With people having to face high taxes and high inflation, and being forced to reduce their savings, there's been a shift of

power into the hands of financial institutions and away from the
real economic sector.

The life assurers and their assets have grown enormously. In
1979, they had total assets of R9,5 billion, which was pretty
much in line those of building societies. But by 1989, life
assurers' assets were R95 billion and those of building societies
just R30 billion. So there's been an enormous shift in the pattern
of savings, into equity-linked investments and away from traditional discretionary forms of savings.

An unhealthy concentration of power?

The factors I've mentioned have, in turn, led to an enormous
increase in the concentration of power and control in the hands
of the big six financial conglomerates. They've been chasing
after paper, so even as the level of fixed investment has declined
by 30%, there has been a boom on the Johannesburg Stock
Exchange.

This raises serious questions about social upliftment.

How do we pay for that 50% addition to the state budget,
when so little has gone into creating the social infrastructure and
more and more money has been bottled up in the financial
sector? How do we reconcile the real needs of the people and
the enormous amount of cash that has been building up in the
financial institutions?

It would be easy to say: "Break up the financial institutions,
break up the conglomerates, tax them to the hilt." But that
doesn't really hit at the fundamental causes of the growth in
concentration.

The underlying causes have been the rise in inflation and the
high personal income tax structure; and the reason for these
problems has been the massive growth in government spending.

The costly bureaucracy

During the 1980s, key sectors of South African industry —
mining, construction, manufacturing, transport and communication — all saw a decline in the level of employment. By contrast,

employment in central government rose by nearly 60% and employment in the local administration of the homelands grew by nearly 40%.

There's been a huge distortion in the structure of the economy, with more and more power going into the hands of the government and more involvement by the government in economic policy. Apartheid ideology has created a massive increase in bureaucracies.

A bureaucratic nightmare

We all know about the huge number of different government departments in the health field, in housing, and in education. There are 19 education departments and 14 health departments, and anyone trying to build a township has to deal with 12 departments of housing.

All this has cost an enormous amount of money. But it gives us a number of options for financing social upliftment.

The first is for government to create a constitution that is far less burdensome to the public and that will save us money. A unitary government could potentially cut the cost of bureaucracy by around R6 billion per annum. In addition — presuming we have a peaceful settlement of regional problems — it should be possible to save another R2 billion in the defence budget. The total saving of R8 billion per annum would be about 11% of South Africa's total annual budget.

Of course, while making an extremely useful contribution, that doesn't come anywhere near to providing the 50% of government budget needed for social upliftment. So what are the other alternatives?

Paying our way

One way for government to raise money is through higher taxation. But people have already been taxed to the hilt. And although the ANC is hell-bent on trying to increase taxation as a way to redistribute income, that would kill the goose that lays the golden egg.

The next possibility is an increase in public debt. We could simply go out and borrow money. However, if foreigners started lending us money to pump into social upliftment, we'd face a rising interest bill. And we've already seen an enormous increase in South Africa's public debt over the last 15 years.

In 1975 interest on government debt accounted for 5% of government expenditure. By 1990, it had increased to 16%. If the process kept going, it would eventually account for 50% or more. Then — as we have seen in South America — the temptation would be to print money. That, in turn, would lead to hyper-inflation and to civil unrest.

Worse, in a hyper-inflationary situation the inequality of income distribution would be exacerbated, not reduced. The rich would get even richer — and the poor would lose out very badly.

Forcing institutions to pay for upliftment

It's been suggested that another way to raise money for social upliftment would be to introduce prescribed asset requirements and to force the financial institutions to pump money into key programmes.

The ANC is now pressing for such solutions.

In its recent economic policy document, it suggested that the institutions should be forced to put a certain proportion of their cash into public housing. This is not unlike the qualification of the mortgages allocated to the SA Housing Trust a few years ago.

The privatisation option

I am very sceptical about any rules and regulations that force things on anyone. Instead of forcing financial institutions to put their money into certain ventures, we could encourage them to do so voluntarily through privatisation. That way, we'd kill two birds with one stone.

The ANC argues that privatisation would lead to an even greater concentration of power. I say that with a bit of ingenuity,

it could become a way to spread public participation and ownership.

A classic case would be in the field of housing. Can we really
afford R5 billion per annum to supply houses to everyone?
Should we even try?

Frankly, I don't think it's feasible. Our priority should be to
provide sites and services for the 60%-odd of our population
who really need decent shelters. At least let them have potable
water, adequate sanitation, and the like. To achieve this, Government could, for example, use the R3 billion it realised from
the sale of ISCOR.

The nationalisation threat

There are a number of problems with nationalisation.

First, how would you pay for the assets of the Old Mutual,
Sanlam, Anglo American, and the like? Where would the money
come from?

Second, nationalisation creates the very bureaucracy that has
led to the decline of the South African economy over the last 20
years. (And the ANC says it favours a less bloated civil service.)

Third, it would be tempting to milk the total cash flow of
nationalised institutions, and to pump the money into upliftment
programmes. So there would be nothing left behind to generate
additional capital.

Financing the future

The fundamental objective of capitalism is to get a return, to use
part of that return, and to plough the remainder back into the
creation of still more capital.

Nationalisation puts an end to the generation of new capital.
Through privatisation, however, the financial institutions would
indirectly put their money into social upliftment. And they'd get
a return on those projects which could be used to generate new
capital along the way.

I believe the ANC is totally misguided in suggesting that
through nationalisation it could redistribute income more equit-

ably. On the contrary, nationalisation would result in more government involvement, higher taxation, and higher inflation; the end result would be even greater inequality in the distribution of income.

What it all leads to

There are enormous opportunities ahead of us, but there are enormous costs, too. Until we can find ways to pump money into upliftment programmes in a non-inflationary way, the opportunities will not materialise.

The biggest danger for South Africa in the 1990s is hyperinflation as we try to address our problems. In the light of high interest rates and the downward trend of the business cycle, unemployment will probably grow fast. So the possibility of more violence is very real, in the short term at least. Longer-term, a number of factors — including the lifting of sanctions — will give us some breathing space. From the second half of 1991, the economy could start recovering and the pattern of violence should diminish.

After that, as more and more people are exposed to opportunities, more opportunities will present themselves.

But there's one proviso. Until the mass of people are educated enough to understand the workings of this economy, I don't think we should be over-optimistic. And educating all our people is going to take time. So I think that the really rapid growth that South Africa might experience will only come in the first decade of the 21st Century.

Chapter Five
THE ANGRY YOUTH

JOHN KANE-BERMAN

John Kane-Berman is Executive Director of the South African Institute of Race Relations, and is well known both in SA and internationally for his role in raising that organisation's profile. He has also been extensively involved in NEST and in the KwaZulu Natal Indaba. He has delivered papers on the changing face of SA in Australia, the United Kingdom, Western Europe, the Soviet Union, and the United States of America. He is the author of several books, including the definitive study of the 1976 upheaval in Soweto, and *South Africa's Silent Revolution* (Southern Book Publishers 1990).

Rapid urbanisation and population growth mean that there has been a large increase in the number of young Africans in South Africa's cities and towns. In the last 15 years, black youth have played a leading role in political action. High levels of frustration and expectations among them combine to make them a potentially explosive factor that threatens stability. How many people are we talking about?

According to Urban Foundation research, there are currently 1,8 million Africans between the ages of 10 and 24 in urban areas within the homelands, and 2,5 in such areas outside of the homelands, giving a total of 4,3 million.

The 1985 figure was 3,5 million, so the number of urban black youths is growing by about 165 000 a year. Nearly one-third of all urban Africans are either teenagers or young adults. A great many of them are neither studying nor working.

Rising unemployment

The economics unit of Bankorp reported recently that practically no new jobs were created in the formal sector of the South African economy in the 1980s, and that unemployment had risen "especially sharply" among new entrants to the labour market.[8]

Sanlam says that more than half of all unemployed Africans (excluding the TBVC territories) are under the age of 30.[9] One survey showed that in Port Elizabeth, nearly 70% of unemployed blacks are 35 years of age or younger.[10] The Inkatha Institute suggests that 75% of the youth in Natal are unemployed.[11]

How great unemployment is across the country, has long been a matter of dispute. The National Manpower Commission has estimated it at about one million, but says the figure would be three million if those in subsistence farming and the informal sector who want formal sector jobs were to be included.

8 Bankorp economic unit: Econovision, third quarter 1990
9 Sanlam economic research department: Economic Survey, October 1989;
   Cape Times, quoting the October economic review of Sanlam
10 *Eastern Province Herald*, 14 June 1990
11 *Business Day*, 7 May 1990

The Development Bank of Southern Africa recently estimated that 42% of the country's potential workforce does not have formal employment opportunities.[12] According to the Minister of Health and Population Development, with a population increase rate of 2,3% a year, South Africa needs to maintain a real growth rate of 5% per annum to be able to provide work for the 1 000-odd people entering the labour market each day.

In other words, the economic growth rate needs to be double the population growth rate. In the past decade, however, the economy has grown at only half the rate at which the population has grown. No wonder that the Minister of Manpower said in October 1987 that up to six million South Africans could be unemployed by the year 2000; or that the Minister of Finance in the KwaZulu administration said in his budget speech in May this year, that 70% of the economically active population in the Durban functional region would be unemployed by the year 2000.[13] Very large numbers of these will be younger people.

Can the informal sector deliver?

Will the informal sector come to the rescue?

It's been suggested that of the 350 000 people joining the labour market each year, 150 000 join the informal sector and 100 000 the small business (assets below R1,5m) sector. The other 100 000 go into big business or public sector employment, or remain jobless.[14]

The size of the black informal sector has been a source of dispute and speculation for several years. The results of the first official comprehensive survey of this sector were published in March 1990 by the Central Statistical Service. The value of informal sector production in 1989 was found to be about R16 billion — equivalent to 7,3% of gross domestic product (GDP) of R202 billion (excluding the four independent homelands).

12 *Star*, 25 September 1990
13 *Natal Mercury*, 10 May 1990
14 Roots of Enterprise, Small Business Development Corporation, a *Leadership* publication, June 1988, p. 72

According to the survey, 2,6 million Africans worked in the informal sector. Nearly two-thirds of these were full-time workers; the remainder were housewives or schoolchildren, who were active in this sector on a part-time basis. One in every 13 coloured, one in every seven Indian, and one in every four African workers worked in the informal sector.[15]

Without the presence of the informal sector in some black townships and shantytowns, the situation of people there would be desperate. Many people are believed to start their own businesses in the informal sector simply to survive.[16] Rapid black urbanisation, the decline in agricultural employment, and stagnation elsewhere have stimulated this "survival entrepreneurship."

However, officials of the South African Reserve Bank believe it would be a mistake to present the informal economy as a major success story. In their view, the growth of the black informal sector reflects joblessness arising from the low growth of the formal sector.[17]

This is presumably the reason why the KwaZulu Natal region generates only about 16% of South Africa's GDP,[18] but accounts for one-third of all informal sector activity among blacks. Nearly 40% of all such activity is in the six non-independent homelands.

According to the Inkatha Institute, the informal sector in Durban and Pietermaritzburg has become overtraded.[19] The implication of all this is that this sector will not absorb entrants to the labour market to the extent it has done in the past.

15 Central Statistical Service, Statistical Newsletter: Statistically Unrecorded Economic Activities of Coloureds, Indians, and Blacks, October 1989, 20 March 1990
16 Finance Week, 9–15 April 1987
17 Observation made at a seminar of the Economic Society of South Africa, Johannesburg branch, 20 March 1990
18 Business Day, 2 May 1990
19 Business Day, 7 May 1990

The failure of education

If neither the formal nor the informal economy can absorb black youth, what about the education system?

Ideally, all youngsters of school-going age should be in class. According to various estimates, however, between one-third and one-half of the Africans of that age have either dropped out or have never attended school.

The high drop-out rate in black schools meant that in 1989 there were about 150 000 black pupils in matric; there would have been 450 000 if the progression rate from grade one to matric had been the same for blacks as for whites.[20] However, whereas 78% of the whites who entered grade one in 1978 were in matric in 1989, the black proportion was only 25%.

According to one survey[21] poverty is by far the major reason why so many children drop out of school; but boycotts and other disruptions of the black schooling system have also contributed to this state of affairs.

In the view of one seasoned observer, "national academic genocide" is being committed by people who "do not have their own children in the schools they are disrupting. Their children are in elite private schools in this country and overseas. . . . The enslavement they are visiting upon a generation of young people is many times worse than what apartheid has done during the past 42 years of National Party rule."[22]

Money hasn't solved the problem

Black education could almost be described as a disaster area — despite major efforts by the government to improve it, dating back to the early 1970s.

20 Senbank: Focus on key economic issues, Number 46, June 1990
21 *Star*, 7 September 1990
22 Dr Oscar Dhlomo, *Ilanga*, 21–23 June 1990

Between 1971/72 and 1987/88, state spending on African education went up by nearly 6 000%, from R70 million to R4 097 million.[23] Twenty years ago the government was spending 18 times as much on a white as on an African pupil.[24] As a result of the greater allocations to Africans since then, the ratio dropped to about 4,6:1 in 1987/88 (outside the homelands, where the gap has narrowed much less).[25]

As a result of the government's attempts to reduce the drop-out rate, African secondary school enrolment has been growing by about 8% a year since the early 1970s. A few years ago, the number of Africans matriculating caught up with the number of whites (between 53 000 and 54 000), and by the end of the century, seven out of every 10 matriculants will be African.[26]

These figures are impressive, but many black matriculants are already unemployable and their numbers will grow.

Too much time on the wrong subjects

Although there has been a large increase in the number of Africans matriculating (despite high failure rates), only a miniscule proportion obtain university entrance passes in mathematics. In the Johannesburg area, for example, only 41 of the 1 558 Africans who wrote higher-grade mathematics in 1987 passed it. The vast majority of African pupils do not even study maths or physical science.

Professor J P de Lange, who headed an investigation into South African education for the Human Sciences Research Council, says that 80% of children at white secondary schools and 99% at black secondary schools are taking academic subjects, when the figure should be about 30%. The other pupils

23 1971 Survey, p. 252; 1988/89 Survey, p. 244
24 John Kane-Berman, *Soweto: Black Revolt, White Reaction*, Ravan Press, Johannesburg, 1978, p. 187
25 1988/89 Survey, p. 245
26 John Kane-Berman, *South Africa's Silent Revolution*, South African Institute of Race Relations and Southern Book Publishers, Johannesburg and Halfway House, 1990, p. 8

need to take courses directed at business and technical needs, he says.

In short, there's a mismatch between the skills the economy requires and those produced by the education system.

The chairman of the Electricity Council reported in March 1990 that the mismatch resulted in about 80 000 matriculants being unemployed in 1988.[27] At the same time, South Africa faces a huge unemployment problem, and a serious shortage of skilled labour. According to one estimate, we will have a surplus of more than nine million semi-skilled and unskilled people by the year 2000 and a shortage of 200 000 skilled workers.[28]

South Africans of all races have an elitist idea of education; vocational and technical education is regarded as *infra dig*. So the ambition of most young people and their parents is for them to go to universities rather than technikons. Australia has 800 000 students in technical education, but South Africa, with double the population, just 60 000.

According to Dr Jan Visser, Executive Director of the National Productivity Institute, some 60% of German school leavers go on to a technical career, whereas in South Africa the figure is around 11%.[29]

Our university population is growing faster than the technikon population, which should not be the case. Yet only 1% of black students are interested in a technical education.

Is there an answer?

We seem to be in a "Catch-22" situation. Such qualified manpower as is being produced does not have the skills required to help the economy grow more quickly; but the economy can't grow more quickly unless we have more people with the right skills.

Yet one suspects that any attempt by the government to make education more appropriate to the economy's needs may be

27 *Citizen*, 30 March 1990
28 Institute for Futures Research at the University of Stellenbosch, quoted in
   1988/89 Survey, p. 406
29 *Financial Mail*: A special report on South African Technikons, 7 April 1989

resisted. Scarce resources, once squandered on apartheid, may continue to be spent on the kind of education system that is irrelevant to our greatest need of all: to achieve and sustain a rate of economic growth fast enough to mop up unemployment, and so eliminate poverty from this country.

The phenomenon of too many matriculants chasing too few jobs is explosive. Indeed, the resulting frustration is the underlying cause of the black youth rebellion that has kept black townships on the boil for most of the last 15 years.

What chance of a job?

In retrospect, one could argue that the turning point in modern South African history was not 1990, but 1970 — when the surplus of skilled white labour dried up for the first time. Then, the government had reluctantly acknowledged that the country would have to rely more and more on black manpower to keep the economy growing at the rate of 6% a year. This had been achieved in the 1960s, and had mopped up all the available white skills.

Prime Minister Vorster accordingly sounded the retreat from the industrial colour bar, and his government began to put more money into black education. The notorious white/black per capita state education spending ratio peaked at 18:1 at the beginning of the 1970s, and has been shrinking ever since.

But the cruel hand of fate intervened.

Just as the State started spending more on black education — especially secondary schooling — to meet the economy's needs, the rate of GDP growth slowed dramatically. The 6% average of the 1960s was halved in the 1970s, and halved again in the 1980s.[30] Because employment has failed to keep pace with the rapid growth in African secondary school enrolment, the chances of finding a job of a given standard with a given educational attainment have dropped quite markedly.

---

30 1987/88 Survey, p. 406

Unemployment leads to violence

Professor Charles Simkins observes that the emergence of unemployment among senior secondary school leavers, combined with continuing inequality of opportunity, has proved a powerfully destabilising mix. Small wonder, he says, that black youth has been in the vanguard of every political challenge to state authority.

The first time this happened was in 1976, when Soweto and 160 other black communities around the country erupted in revolt. At the end of 1975, the number of black matriculants grew by 36% — only to coincide with the re-appearance of unemployment in the urban areas.[31] The education/employment gap has helped to keep black townships on the boil since September 1984, when the present wave of violence began.

Despite school disruptions, the number of black matriculants doubled between 1984 and 1989 (from 42 000 to 82 000 — although growth was not steady, but erratic). The correlation between political turbulence (as measured by fatality statistics) and unemployment appears to hold good for this period.

Fatalities increased in 1985 and 1986. They then declined in 1987 and 1988, when unemployment also declined (outside the independent homelands, at any rate). In 1989, both violence and unemployment rose again.

Sanlam may thus be correct in its view that "the areas where unrest-related incidents occur most often also have the highest unemployment rates in South Africa.[32]

The politicised education system

Government has at long last recognised the huge damage that Bantu Education has inflicted, not only on education itself, but on the economy and on race relations as well. The iron grip of apartheid on South African education has been prised loose and the system is being steadily desegregated, less because of than in spite of the government.

31 Kane-Berman, Soweto, pp. 48–49
32 Sanlam, ibid

But education is now more politicised than ever. It has fallen prey to the all-or-nothing ethic that is so prevalent in township politics. The government is now in danger of being caught up in a situation where every concession it makes simply leads to demands for further concessions.

Mr Sam Mabe, late assistant editor of the *Sowetan*, put it this way:

"We requested the building of more classrooms and the repair of the damaged ones. The Minister heeded our call and met teachers' representatives. A great percentage of our other demands have been addressed or are being addressed and we were happy to see teachers going back to school. But their conditions for returning were, among other things, that they would not engage in extra-mural activities organised by the DET or non-examination subjects. Also, they want principals to be engaged in full-time teaching. This doesn't make sense. What alternative programme are they providing to ensure that the wheels of learning will not stop turning?

Quite rightly, we have serious problems with our education. But taking punitive or spiteful action instead of corrective action can only make us feel good that we are frustrating the government, but frustrating the government as an end in itself can only benefit all but our children. And heaven help us all if our objective is to make schools ungovernable, for we could be starting what we may not be able to end. We are creating a culture we will not require in a post-apartheid society."

It is clear that very large numbers of black youngsters are not spending their waking hours where they should: in school or at work. Nor does any short-term relief appear to be in sight.

Recipe for instability

Many educational and other grievances remain, so education will continue to be a focus for political action. Monetary policy designed to bring down the rate of inflation and protect our foreign reserves will inevitably ensure that the labour absorption rate of the economy remains below the growth rate of the workforce.

Political instability and general uncertainty about this country's short- and medium-term future will also help to keep the economic growth rate down. It seems doubtful that much foreign investment will come into South Africa in the immediate future, even if foreign economic sanctions were to be lifted tomorrow. The situation of urban black youth is both ironic and tragic. It is ironic that all efforts of the government to deal with the backlogs in black education, including huge increases in expenditure, have also been a recipe for greater instability. Black youth have remained politically fired up since the Soweto revolt against Bantu education in particular, and apartheid in general.

Black youth are absolutely determined that they will not live out their lives under the system of apartheid, as so many of their parents did. They're not only prepared to die for the struggle as hundreds — if not thousands — have done; some are also prepared to kill for it.

The young revolutionaries

Today's activist youth is very different from his or her 1976 counterpart. Then, schoolchildren coerced rank-and-file black people into complying with stayaways and boycotts in both Soweto in August 1976, and in Guguletu and Nyanga (Cape Town) in December of that year. Hostel dwellers counter-attacked when schoolchildren tried to enforce obedience to stayaways from work.[33]

Then, as now, there were allegations of police involvement on the side of the hostel dwellers. It was notable, however — particularly after the conflict between hostel dwellers and householders in Soweto in 1976, in which 70 people died — that schoolchildren attempted to win the hostel dwellers over to their side, instead of trying to use force against them. Today's activist, by contrast, uses coercion almost as a matter of course.

33 Kane-Berman, Soweto, pp. 5–6, 113–114, 130–132

Class of '76

A great many youngsters fled Soweto after a reign of terror by the police. They eventually found their way into ANC training camps. The revolt of the mid-1970s was a black consciousness-inspired phenomenon, but youngsters who fled the townships found that the only organisation with the resources to receive them in exile was the ANC.

Some of these youngsters subsequently came back, having received military training abroad. More of them will no doubt return under the agreements between the government and the ANC. A leaflet put out by the Soweto Students' Representative Council calling for a five-day stayaway in November 1976 read as follows:

AZIKHWELWA

1. From Monday 1st - 5th November, 1976
2. INSTRUCTIONS:
   (a) All workers stay at home for 5 days.
   (b) Nurses and doctors to go on with their daily routine work.
   (c) Black provision stores (grocers, butchers, dairies) open from 8 am to 12 noon daily during the stay-at-home.
   (d) No shebeen drinking — All shebeens should close down.
   (e) No purchase from white shops for the whole week.
   (f) Parents, workers and all schoolchildren must remain indoors, and avoid standing in groups on the streets.
   (g) Workers should do their best to obey this call, so as to avoid violence and bloodshed.
   (h) Hostel residents should also stay in their hostels — be careful of police agitators. Do not be incited into fighting your people.
   (i) Tsotsis please do not rob people (Geen Bulvangery).
   (j) Churches and families should hold prayers in commemoration of black children who have been shot and killed by police all over the country (31.10.76).
   (k) The Stay-at-Home shall be non-violent and peaceful. NO CHRISTMAS SHOPPING OF ANY KIND

NO CHRISTMAS CARDS AND DECORATIONS
NO CHRISTMAS PARTIES
BLACKS ARE GOING INTO MOURNING FOR THEIR
DEAD
3. VORSTER & KRUGER:
   (a) Resign, you have mismanaged Azania. You have
   plunged the country into violence and loss of human
   life.
   (b) Release all detainees.
   (c) Police, remain in your barracks and please behave.
   We are determined to free ourselves from the shackles
   of the oppressor.
THE STRUGGLE IS ON !
N.B. This call is National.
BLACK PEOPLE LET US BE ONE !
UNITED WE STAND !
VICTORY IS OURS !

(Issued by: Soweto Students' Representative Council)

Are they listening to their leaders?

Both the tone and the content of that 1976 leaflet are strikingly
different from those of a newspaper advertisement published in
June 1990 by the South African Youth Congress (Sayco), in
connection with a call for the commemoration of June 16, 1976:

On that historic day, June 16, 1976, the youth of South Africa
selflessly and defiantly took to the streets to demonstrate their
arch hatred of Bantu Education. This year, the celebration of
June 16 takes place at a time when our people, led by the
ANC, are at the threshold of victory and the question of the
transferral of power into the hands of the people is on the
immediate agenda. Sayco calls upon the youth to assert
themselves more than ever before in the forward march to
freedom and:
• build and strengthen the fighting formations of the people,
  the ANC, SACP, Cosatu and UMKHONTO WE SIZWE.
  Added to this the youth is urged to support and defend the
  initiatives that are taken by our leaders to take the struggle

to a higher level and achieve an urgent and peaceful solution to the problems of the country.
Sayco has declared June 1990 the "MONTH OF THE YOUTH". In line with the adopted programme for this month we are urging the youth to play an active role in the organisation of June 16 rallies and in their thousands attend the rallies that are organised by Sayco to celebrate this day (details of which will be disclosed at a later date); to ensure that the national blitz campaign of massive recruitment for the ANC from June 17–25 is a success, and to creatively celebrate June 26, South African Freedom Day and popularise the Freedom Charter.
The student youth must, through their organisations, intensify the struggle for a non-racial and democratic education system. In the same breath these compatriots must occupy their fighting trenches, the universities, colleges and schools, build organs of popular rule like SRCs and PTSAs and through them implement Peoples Education.
"ALL TO BATTLE — ALL TO OUR TRENCHES"
"ATTEND ALL SAYCO JUNE 16 RALLIES"
"FORWARD TO ANC YOUTH LEAGUE"
"FORM DEFENCE UNITS"

Earlier in 1990, Sayco issued a call to "Mobilise, organise for the final offensive! All youth to the battle! All youth to the frontline!" Sayco is closely involved in the re-establishment of the ANC's youth league inside the country. The league is planning to hold a congress in April 1991.[34]

The behaviour of youth activists evidently alarmed Mr Nelson Mandela sufficiently for him to appeal for tolerance at a Sayco congress in April 1990. He said: "You are expected to respect other freedom fighters outside our movement. Those who do not agree with us must be allowed the freedom to propagate their ideas freely."

City Press praised Mr Mandela's call as timely and appropriate, and reminded its readers that it was the youth who "introduced the necklace method of killing."[35] (Since Septem-

34 Beeld, 10 October 1990
35 City Press, 15 April 1990

ber 1984, some 850 people have died by necklace murders or other burnings.) However, Mr Mandela's call was not enough to discourage Sayco from declaring Chief Mangosuthu Buthelezi an enemy of the people.[36]

"Shocktroops" of the revolution

It is frequently argued that activist youth are beyond the control of the leadership. But one needs to ask to what extent leadership has actually attempted to control them. The kind of language that organisations like Sayco use is seldom repudiated by people to whom they presumably look for leadership.

Sayco leaders have referred to themselves as "shocktroops." The organisation's president, Mr Peter Mokaba, told Mr Mandela: "We are your stormtroopers."[37]

Sayco embraces high school pupils, students, and unemployed youth. It is not the only youth organisation in South Africa, although with 1,5 million members, it claims to be the biggest. The Inkatha youth brigade, with half that membership, would then be the second biggest.

Youth organisations also operate in the Africanist and black consciousness camps. Members of most, if not all, of these various organisations have been involved in violent conflict with one another, showing that political intolerance is a major problem in black communities.

Development of a black underclass

Violence has many other causes, among them the education/employment gap already mentioned. Poverty and malnutrition, the have/have-not gap within black communities, poor housing and social services, and a host of other factors all contribute to instability in South Africa. We are probably seeing the development of a black underclass of sizeable proportions.

36 *New Nation*, 20–26 April 1990
37 *South African Update*, 1–30 April 1990

Black youth have also been the victims of detention without trial, indiscriminate and unjustified police shootings, and violence inflicted by one another.

Recently, two teenagers were necklaced near Vanderbijlpark, apparently by other youths. In mid-1990, a 12-year-old was necklaced in Natal.[38] The fact that a couple of dozen black youths could so easily be recruited by an apparently disturbed man for a stabbing rampage against whites on the Durban beachfront recently, suggests that apartheid has bred a kind of counter-hatred.

Quite obviously, as in 1976, so-called "tsotsis" are involved in intimidation, crime, and violence.[39]

UDF officials have claimed that some "tsotsis" wear political T-shirts and then perpetrate violence.[40] There is no doubt truth in this. But at the same time, it is clear that instability also arises in situations of deliberate political action which cannot be dismissed as the work of "tsotsis."

Mass action

Black youth play a major role in mass action, which is a major component of ANC strategy. Indeed, given the erosion of international economic sanctions and the failure down the years of "armed struggle" waged from neighbouring states, mass mobilisation is becoming a dominant ANC strategy.

Mass mobilisation encompasses general strikes and stayaways, rent and consumer boycotts, and school boycotts and disruptions. Stayaways and boycotts are now the order of the day.

The South African Communist Party proclaims that the government may control the formal machinery of the state but that the "people" control the streets. Many of these "people" — probably most of them — are activist youths.

Explaining the Pretoria Minute of August 6, 1990, the ANC said in an advertisement that suspending the armed struggle

38 *Star*, 8 October 1990
39 *South Africa Update*, 1–30 April 1990
40 *South Africa Update*, 1–30 April 1990

meant that the organisation "will not carry out any further armed actions and related activities such as the infiltration of armed cadres and weaponry." The advertisement added that the "armed struggle has not been abandoned" and that "Umkhonto we Sizwe has not been dissolved." Under a heading "mass action continues," it said: "mass struggles have to continue in all spheres of our lives to achieve our objective of a united non-racial democratic and non-sexist society."

High stakes in the power game

Mass mobilisation carries very high risks. One is the obvious risk of confrontation with an undisciplined police force which all too often has opened fire as a first, rather than as a last, resort.

Another risk is that of conflict between the organisers of mass mobilisation and rank-and-file township people.

The right to protest is an important democratic right. But boycotts and stayaways are now almost routinely imposed without prior consultation of the people expected to comply with them. Frequently, people have been coerced into supporting consumer boycotts — most notoriously by being forced to drink detergent and cooking oil. Sometimes people not complying with boycotts have been forced to eat newspapers they were told not to buy, or plastic milk bottles. One man in the Orange Free State was forced to swallow a bottle of pills he had bought during a boycott. He died from the overdose.

I suspect that the extent of coercion used to back stayaways and other mass action has been seriously under-reported by both the South African and the foreign press — partly because many newspapers do not want to cast political groups organising mass action in a bad light, and partly because black journalists covering township politics fear for their own lives if they expose this violent coercion.

The spark that ignites conflict .

Most of the political violence that South Africa has seen since the initial outbreak in September 1984 has occurred in situations of mass mobilisation. Why has mass mobilisation been stepped up at a time when the government has been lifting political restrictions?

A possible answer may be found in a meeting of the ANC, the UDF, and Cosatu in July 1989, where the fear was expressed that the government might attempt to blunt the struggle with a strategy of negotiation.

Mass mobilisation was seen as a means of pre-empting government strategies and preventing it from taking the political initiative. Accordingly, the meeting resolved to "fend off" government initiatives through a programme of action "capable of firing up the imagination of the people and building up action to increasingly higher levels."

On February 2, 1990, the government did indeed seize the initiative. Mass mobilisation continues as the ANC camp attempts to wrest it back.

At a "conference for a democratic future," organised by the ANC and the UDF at the University of the Witwatersrand in December 1989, a call was made "to mobilise our forces, to organise and intensify the struggle." Objectives included launching mass-based campaigns, working towards dismantling the "puppet structures" of local government, and initiating a process leading to the dismantling of all "bantustans."

Most newspapers reported this as if the call had been merely to organise a series of cake sales around the country. But it is necessary to examine what such calls mean in practice.

The unhappy lot of town councillors

In April 1990, it was reported that about 10% of the black town councillors in the Transvaal had resigned as a result of intimidation, violence, and other pressure from extra-parliamentary organisations demanding the abolition of all apartheid structures. The report said: "They live behind barbed wire. Their cars are petrol-bombed, their houses stoned. Some have suffered gruesome deaths at the hands of angry mobs." Later the same month, it was reported that a 75-year-old councillor had apparently shot and killed himself after firing at a group of youths who stoned him and surrounded his home near Newcastle in Natal. Police said that his body had then been dragged from the house while youths set fire to his home, a motor cycle, two cars, two minibuses, and a garage, and plundered shops he owned.

In August, it was reported that the mayor of Alexandra township near Johannesburg had resigned because her home had been attacked six times with petrol bombs since February.

The campaign against the black local government system is to be renewed. At a press conference in Johannesburg early in November 1990, a new umbrella organisation of 38 civic associations in the Southern Transvaal announced that "mass grassroots struggles and campaigns would be intensified" to force the resignation of local councillors. Boycotts, protest marches, and stayaways were to be among the strategies used.[41]

"The struggle" extends into the homelands

When political upheaval flared up early in 1990 in all four of the independent homelands, as well as in Gazankulu and Lebowa in the Transvaal, an official of the UDF, Mr Patrick Lekota, said: "Our people in the bantustans have learnt from their counterparts in the urban areas who have brought down the councils in wave after wave. They have learnt that these administrations can only be removed by mass action."

It is from mass mobilisation (and the various responses to it), rather than from armed struggle narrowly defined, that chronic instability, political tensions, and violence principally arise in South Africa. Although the government had hoped to obtain a commitment to end mass mobilisation in the Pretoria talks, such mobilisation continues and may indeed be intensified.

Can the ANC stop mass mobilisation?

The government will presumably try in future talks to have mass mobilisation curtailed. But since it is probably the ANC's major

41 *Citizen*, 9 and 10 October, *Star* 9 October 1990

weapon, it's difficult to see how the organisation can abandon it. To do so would weaken its own bargaining position, which it is obviously loath to do — as would be any other organisation in a similar position.

Another risk for the ANC in abandoning mass mobilisation would be to antagonise many of its own supporters, particularly the younger ones.

Continued use of mass mobilisation is a risk for the ANC, however, in that the resulting coercion may antagonise ordinary township people and so erode the ANC's potential support base. Other organisations — among them the National Party — might gain some advantage. The ANC is thus obviously in a difficult position.

The logical consequence of continued mass mobilisation is that activist black youth — whether studying or not, whether employed or not — will remain a destabilising factor in the urban areas (and elsewhere too).

Older political leadership appears to be deeply ambivalent about the role of youth. On the one hand, it calls for discipline, as it has done on more than one occasion; but on the other, it embarks on courses of action in which youth clearly play a major role and routinely use coercive tactics.

At the same time, of course, senior political leadership continues to call for economic sanctions, which is one reason unemployment is as high as it is.

If these leaders were anxious to bring youth under control, they'd surely be a great deal more cautious about using mass mobilisation strategies. Either that, or the youth are not only the shock troops, but also the major influence in strategic decision making.

If that is the case, effective control of the ANC has already passed to the next generation.

Chapter Six

THE LABOUR ICEBERG: REACHING BELOW THE SURFACE

DR JOHAN VAN ZIJL

Dr Johan van Zijl has experience at many levels of
education. He has taught at primary and high
schools and lectured at universities and teacher
education colleges. He was the Principal Education
Planner for the Natal Education Department and is
currently Executive Director of the Education
Foundation, an independent trust committed to the
development of a non-racial system of education
that offers equality of opportunity and access to all.

Education is the most basic and arguably the most important challenge facing the new South Africa. Recent events have shown that it also may prove to be the most difficult to address. Half our adult population is illiterate and half our pupil population is not at school. A major concern is that our already stagnant rate of economic growth will be further eroded by an inadequate supply of wealth-producing technical skills. Even when South Africa rejoins world markets, our capacity to regenerate the economy will be limited by our under-developed human resources.

Distribute opportunity not wealth

Dr Conrad Strauss, Group Managing Director of the Standard Bank, has noted that economic development in Southern Africa has occurred within the political and ideological framework of colonial, post-colonial, and neo-colonial administrations. Governments have channelled resources into those areas which most benefitted the ruling group of the time. As a result, inevitable distortions have been introduced into the economy.

Concurrently, decades of creeping poverty have brought this country to the point where bold and visionary changes are required if our economic potential is ever to be realised. We must spend the next decade building our human capital if we are to secure constant, acceptable economic growth, particularly as our traditional "fallback reserve" of minerals is being overtaken by First World technology.

The decisions we take at this critical point in South Africa's development will have a profound effect on the lives and welfare of our people. We have to plan for success, and we have to appreciate that the long-term cost of inertia can be greater than the short-term cost of action.

Third World reality

As a realistic starting point, we have to accept South Africa's Third World status — particularly in terms of education. But precisely what do we mean by this clichéd term?

Third World countries are characterised by rapid population growth (more than 2% per annum), high illiteracy, and urgent educational needs. Although a large proportion (up to 25%) of the national budget may be devoted to education, the planning, management, and administrative structures are weak and a large proportion of teachers are professionally under-qualified.

Third World countries are further identified by unexploited natural resources, low levels of industrialisation and human resource development, relatively low national incomes, and some dependence on external aid for education and development. South Africa meets all of these criteria.

Author and economist Don Caldwell describes Third World education as authoritarian, top down, state controlled, and stifling; while First World education is characterised by innovation, flexibility, tolerance, and choice. It has nothing to do with race.

It is generally accepted that South Africa's future economic growth potential will be seriously curtailed unless a dramatic shift occurs in the current composition of manpower supply and demand. Figure 6.1 illustrates the size of the problem.

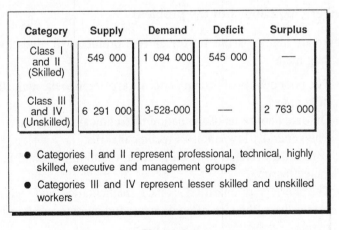

Category	Supply	Demand	Deficit	Surplus
Class I and II (Skilled)	549 000	1 094 000	545 000	—
Class III and IV (Unskilled)	6 291 000	3-528-000	—	2 763 000

● Categories I and II represent professional, technical, highly skilled, executive and management groups

● Categories III and IV represent lesser skilled and unskilled workers

Figure 6.1
MANPOWER SUPPLY AND DEMAND
PROJECTIONS FOR THE YEAR 2000
Source: Bureau for Economic Research, Stellenbosch University

Categories I and II represent professional, technical, highly skilled, executive, and managerial groups. Categories III and IV represent lesser skilled and unskilled workers. These figures confirm an alarming shortage of manpower at the highly-skilled levels which will seriously inhibit the economy's growth performance unless the situation is properly addressed and ameliorated by appropriate policies. (These figures exclude AIDS projections but evidence suggests that AIDS will strike at the economically-active population.)

Business must share responsibility

It would be foolish to expect government alone to solve the problem of skills shortages. It will also be up to business and to all participants in the private sector to seek solutions. This should not be seen as mere altruism or as "guilt money," but rather as a business investment in the creation of skills and markets.

Underlying causes of the problem

There are many reasons for the current problems in education. Among them:

❏ The poor quality of primary education offered to the majority of people
❏ Outdated concepts of the nature of technical education
❏ The generally low status of technical skills
❏ Difficulties related to cultural background and second language learning
❏ The shortage of qualified science, mathematics, and technical teachers, the lack of equipment, and overcrowded classrooms
❏ The absence of career guidance
❏ The "lost generation"
❏ The lack of electricity in schools.

Let's examine each of these issues, and possible remedies.

THE POOR QUALITY OF PRIMARY EDUCATION OFFERED TO THE MAJORITY OF PEOPLE

World Bank studies have shown that better primary school education increases productivity in all sectors of the economy, *and* that the economic returns are greater than from all other levels of schooling. In addition, better primary schooling offers the following benefits:

❑ It reduces fertility
❑ It improves health and nutrition
❑ It promotes positive changes in attitude at both the individual and community levels.

Lifelong learning

If the pre-school environment means so much to the social and personal development of future citizens, and has such significant implications for the political stability and economic status of the country, business must become far more involved.

In South Korea businesses created many pre-primary centres for their workers' children. These were far more than mere care centres — they were incubators for social coordination and creative spirit.

John Naisbitt, author of *Megatrends*, talked of a new buzz word — "TLC." It was essential, he said, for people to learn to Think . . . learn to Learn . . . learn to Create.

This is where countries like South Korea and Singapore built their future success as nations. Many studies have shown that basic primary education is the single best educational investment. Yet in South Africa, one-quarter of black pupils don't progress beyond Grade I/Sub-A.

One out of four pupils fails at the very first hurdle, and goes out into the world without even the most elementary literacy skills. Illiterates are relegated to the most peripheral positions of powerlessness in our society. Nick Taylor of the Education Policy Unit has referred to this drop-out figure as "probably the

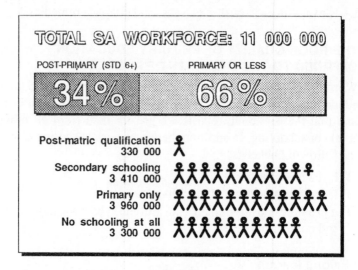

Figure 6.2

largest problem at any level in the South African school system." (Figure 6.2.)

As a matter of urgency we need to re-open the debate on tax concessions for the funding of primary education. At the moment concessions apply only to funding of secondary and tertiary education. Can we afford this situation?

Both management and workers should be encouraged to become directly and actively involved in pre-school provision for children of employees and the wider community. There is much scope here also for union involvement.

OUTDATED CONCEPTS IN TECHNICAL EDUCATION

A strong case needs to be made for the relevance of technical and vocational education in the social reconstruction of South Africa.

Ten years ago, the de Lange Commission recommended the removal of negative connotations associated with the term "vocational education." Perhaps we should act now, and introduce the concept of "career education," emphasising opportunities for life-long education and progress as people advance along their chosen career paths.

THE GENERALLY LOW STATUS OF TECHNICAL SKILLS

Clem Sunter has observed that "one of the terrible legacies of the colonial system is the idea that arts matter more than science and technology."

In spite of many attempts, we've been largely unable to make technical training a sufficiently attractive option. Engineers and technicians must be given the same recognition as lawyers, accountants, and other professionals.

We must recognise and promote the fact that the greatest economic growth rates occur in nations that focus on science and technology. This is not new information, and much has already been said and written about the status of technical education and the need for skills rather than qualifications. But so far the message has had little effect.

The private sector now has a direct responsibility to market the concept of technical education and skills training, and to spell out the opportunities that exist.

The time is also ripe to explore the concept of "magnet schools" of technology, located near key industries.

Magnet schools are government schools that teach the basics, including languages, mathematics, and science. In addition, they offer a specialised curriculum to allow in-depth study of special interest subjects, or the development of special abilities. They try to match learner needs with the learning environment so students are interested in, and motivated by, what they learn.

The unified philosophy of these schools is geared towards an interactive relationship with the workplace which fits with the de Lange Commission's proposal of close links between schools and commerce and industry.

DIFFICULTIES RELATED TO CULTURAL
BACKGROUND AND SECOND LANGUAGE LEARNING

Schooling in a second language — the lot of all black children from the age of about 10 or 11 — is a laborious and inefficient process. It places limitations on the pupil's understanding, since adopting a foreign language tends to cause a duality of thought patterns. The child must modify existing cultural norms and construct new ones, based on values developed by other people with different cultural ideals.

Yet there is growing recognition that economic advancement depends to a great degree on mastery of a world language. It is this belief that has influenced countries such as Namibia to introduce English as the medium of instruction.

English is the most common official world language. Some 80% of information stored in computers is in English. It is undoubtedly the language of business, of industry, and of government. After Mandarin Chinese, it's the language spoken by most people.

But there's strong research evidence to suggest that mother tongue instruction is a critical component of an individual's first school encounters. Also, that the longer the home language is used as the medium of instruction before switching to English, the better the chances of achieving full bilingualism.

This suggests an incremental approach: start teaching all children in their home language and gradually introduce and increase the amount of instruction in English.

Many issues would have to be considered in the adoption of such a language policy. Professor Njabulo Ndebele, Chairman of COSAW, has stressed the possibility that South African English will become a new language rather than being elitist. Jeremy Cronin expressed a similar view at an ANC workshop in Harare:

"If, indeed, English gets to be consolidated as a single national *lingua franca*, then we shall have to practice regicide. The Queen in Queen's English will have to be dethroned and beheaded. The English that we standardise and promote will have to be English in the mouths of the majority of our people.

"The consolidation of a single national *lingua franca* will depend above all on making this *lingua franca* truly available to all South African citizens. A language policy must be an integral component of an education policy in which priority is given to overcoming illiteracy."

In conclusion, it needs to be born in mind that South Africa has no less than 24 languages and that there is a clear need for English to play a vital linking role between our diverse cultures and communities.

THE SHORTAGE OF QUALIFIED SCIENCE, MATHEMATICS, AND TECHNICAL TEACHERS, THE LACK OF EQUIPMENT, AND OVERCROWDED CLASSROOMS

Rapid population growth and poor planning and management in education have led to overcrowded classrooms and laboratories, and a lack of facilities, textbooks, and equipment.

One of the anomalies in teacher training is the fact that changes in schools tend to precede those in teacher training, and that it is not unusual for lecturers in remote teacher training colleges to remain unaware of changes in curricula and textbooks.

Mathematics, science, and technical education should be put at the centre of our education system.

In an analysis of Singapore's education system, Professor James Moulder observed that primary schools there are proud of their ability to teach basic mathematical skills and their use in solving everyday problems. They're also good at teaching scientific thinking. And they explain why a modern economy requires technical skills and thrives on technological innovation.

On a more down-to-earth level, an innovative approach has been adapted in Gazankulu and Venda where mobile mathematics and science units visit schools and colleges and in a practical manner deal with the shortage of qualified teachers and lack of appropriate equipment.

THE ABSENCE OF CAREER GUIDANCE

Career or vocational guidance does not feature at all on many formal school timetables. Teachers aren't qualified to teach guidance and tend to be unaware of opportunities in the fields of science or technology.

The time has come to seriously consider privatisation of guidance in schools. Employers should be involved in career information and guidance programmes. John Maree, Chairman of Eskom, has advocated that "educators and employers should stop doing their own thing" and communicate with each other about realistic career opportunities.

There must also be recognition that self-employment is the fastest growing category of work. The *Fortune* 500 companies in the United States shed 3,5 million jobs in the 1980s as a result of automation and computerisation. Many people who were laid off survived because they had the skills necessary to become entrepreneurs and self-starters.

THE "LOST GENERATION"

However successful we may be in revitalising the existing system, or in transforming it over time, we're still confronted with two generations of black students who have "left" the system, and who are, by and large, unemployable.

Add to their number the students who have somehow made it to matric exemption — but of whom only one in four achieves entrance to tertiary education — and you have a highly variable pool of unemployed discontent.

The time has come to accept the need for a new intermediate level of education. It might better be described as a first step.

The model I have in mind is that of community colleges. Properly developed and designed, such places would address:

❑ Vocational/technical skills training (directed towards local needs)
❑ Literacy and numeracy
❑ A range of one- to two-year diplomas for those students unable to obtain university or technikon entrance

❑ Bridging programmes to prepare candidates for entrance/onward development.

Through a multi-faceted curriculum and approach, such colleges could directly address what is arguably the single greatest pressure point in the education and training system.
Several factors would lead to their success:

❑ They should be rooted in the community
❑ They should learn from experiences elsewhere
❑ They could utilise existing buildings and resources provided electricity was made available.

Community colleges, properly thought through and urgently commissioned, would take some pressure off universities and, to a lesser degree, off technikons.

If universities continue to elevate their entry requirements, the number of disenchanted and unqualified school leavers will continue to grow.

If commerce and industry are to stand a chance of lifting productivity, the labour pool must be empowered with primary and secondary skills.

If existing workers — often functionally illiterate and innumerate — are to realise their potential, some more universal method must be found to educate and train them, regardless of their school leaving level. Community colleges could be part of the answer.

THE LACK OF ELECTRICITY IN SCHOOLS

This is central to everything I have recommended. Three-quarters of black schools do not have access to electricity, yet we expect technical competence and vocationally-oriented curricula, we espouse distance learning, and we fret about the shortage of science pupils.

Provide electricity, and at a single stroke you turn the simplest of schools into a 16-hour-a-day education facility, the basis of a community college after hours, a study and homework

facility for students who simply can't work at home, an adult
literacy centre — and even a community centre.

You could provide — and in many cases restore — some
vestige of civil order and sanity to a community.
Of course, this would be a major capital project. But consider
the effect if key regional industries and business centres were to
turn the provision of power into a local self-help project.

If one did no more than tap off the existing power grid into
nearby schools as a form of inward-looking social investment,
education and training would be revolutionised in the affected
region.

The education we need

Education is a multi-dimensional activity. It is inter-linked with
the wider society, with the process of social change, and with
politics.

We cannot afford to wait for a negotiated political solution
before we improve our education system. We must act now.

The question is, what kind of education is needed to accelerate the development of our scarce human resources? Several
facts are clear:

❏ We must make progress towards employment or self-employment for the whole working population. And we must
  make progress towards eliminating poverty and reducing the
  glaring inequalities in our society.

❏ Comprehensive educational planning must be firmly
  grounded in manpower studies which consider present needs
  for specific jobs, as well as self-employment in urban and
  rural areas. (The present situation, where a driver's licence
  is a far more desirable asset in the search for a job than a
  Standard 10 certificate, is a strong disincentive to learning!)

❏ Curriculum design must draw on the local environment and
  must enable people to acquire transferable skills, abilities,
  and aptitudes. Subjects must be integrated so they can be
  used in the real world.

❏ Both formal and non-formal education and training should be interspersed with work throughout life — i.e., recurrent education must be a strong feature of the system. This implies a good basic education from the ages of six to 13 and a flexible, transferable vocational element afterwards. (Estimates are that non-formal education constitutes roughly half the effort spent on education, yet it rarely gets concerted planning. This, in spite of the fact that it is more directly and immediately related to development and careers.)

The situation is really very simple: if education is inadequate, there will be insufficient skills. Without enough skills, the economy will not grow. If that happens, it'll be increasingly difficult to provide the basic necessities of life for more and more people.

Professor Andre du Preez puts it like this: "Not only do educated people make better things, they also make things better and buy better things."

The best way to predict the future is to invent it. We now have the opportunity to do just that.

Chapter Seven
EDUCATION AND TECHNOLOGY: PROSPECTS AND POSSIBILITIES

PROFESSOR CHRISTO VILJOEN

Professor Christo Viljoen is Dean of the Faculty of Engineering of the University of Stellenbosch and Chairman of the Board of the South African Broadcasting Corporation. An electronics engineer, his interest in the promotion of science and technology is evident from his involvement as a Council member of the South African Bureau of Standards and the South African Council for Professional Engineers, his initiative in establishing the Stellenbosch Technopark, and his contribution to the founding of Afrotech.

E ducation is often seen as a panacea for all kinds of societal problems. This is clear from the following statement by W. Brezinka (1981:2):

"When someone wants to do something for peace, he demands 'peace education'; when someone needs to improve public health, then 'health education'; the citizen who wishes to protect or clean up the environment speaks out for 'ecological education'; the person wanting to reduce the number of traffic accidents recommends 'traffic safety education.' We read about 'work education.' 'Education' is offered to people in every level of society. We find infant education, senior citizen education, family education, school education and factory education, prison education and military education, special education for the retarded and the gifted, mass education and elite education."

The educational scene in South Africa has evoked much reaction over the past 15 years, as the country's education, training, and manpower situation has grown steadily more critical.

However, education cannot function within a vacuum. It is in constant interaction with various other forces which operate within the community. And South Africa is today characterised by change in virtually all spheres. Turbulence and transition have been experienced in economics, politics, and society.

The year 1990 will long be remembered as the start of the journey towards the "new South Africa." Progress along that path demands that drastic and urgent steps be taken to alleviate the educational crisis which is crippling our country.

Unfortunately, the whole question of education has been used to further political objectives. It is used, as Michael O'Dowd, Chairman of the Anglo American and De Beers Chairman's Fund, rightly says, "for the purpose of what is euphemistically known as political mobilisation, to turn the majority of people into the tools of those who claim to be their leaders. . . ."

The educational crisis calls for major changes and a restructuring of the educational system. Every person and business in South Africa is affected by the crisis especially in black education.

Symptoms and causes of the education crisis

There are many reasons for the current problems in education. Among them:

❑ The heterogeneous nature of the population. Different interest groups have different expectations. Often within an interest group there are various individuals with conflicting demands or ideas.

❑ The emergence of black consciousness, which schools have to allow, but which is at the same time seen as a symbol of white domination.

❑ Frustration that arises when schooling creates expectations that cannot be realised in the career situation.

❑ Black children, especially, are generally not ready for school at the time of school entry. A major reason is that the environment of pre-school children doesn't support their later learning experiences. Poverty, poor social conditions, and poor day care conditions all contribute to this state of affairs.

❑ Black South Africans have never been allowed to participate in the election of the central government. As a result, they've never had a chance to decide on the education of their children, so they're alienated from the education system.

❑ There is unequal per capita expenditure on education.

❑ Tribal life is in a state of flux and transition. Traditional ways, based on tribal experience and culture, are no longer adequate or capable of providing satisfactory solutions to problems now being encountered by detribalised people, particularly those who have moved away from their tribal lands. The cultural environment in black society does not always prepare them adequately for the demands made upon them by a western school system. Presently, we are not producing education that is culturally acceptable to all people.

❑ A world of work that demands practical skills from the majority, and "centres of excellence" for the academic minority.

❑ A critical shortage of well-qualified teachers. The
pupil:teacher ratio for more than 80% of our pupils is in
excess of 40:1. Many pupils are being taught by teachers with
Standard Eight certificates. Only 3,4% of all black teachers
have degrees. 30% of all black teachers in the RSA have not
passed matric.

❑ A critical shortage of training facilities for teachers. To reach
a national pupil:teacher average of 30:1, 50 000 new teachers
must be employed per year. We simply do not have the
teachers' training colleges or the finances to achieve this.

❑ Inadequate funds. To achieve parity and allow for expansion,
the education budget must be doubled or even trebled. At
present, South Africa spends 18% of GNP on education —
one of the highest ratios in the world — yet expenditure
would have to be increased to 47% of GNP if the educational
standards of white schools were to be extended to all schools.
This is clearly an unattainable target.

❑ More than 20% of black pupils leave school without having
passed Sub A. Only 55% of black pupils reach Standard 4,
and a meagre 15% reach Standard 10 — while 73% of white
pupils reach matric (Institute of Futures Research: University of Stellenbosch).

❑ A bias towards university-based academic education. One
alarming consequence is that demand for university places
will increase by some 750 000 over the next ten years. This
will require the erection of 20 new universities of 20 000
students each.

Another result of the bias towards academic education is
a shortage of people with technical and professional skills.
This leads to imbalances which, in turn, cause serious unemployment. It is ironical that we should have an oversupply of
unemployed graduates, when there's such an urgent need in
South Africa for technicians, technologists, engineers, and
the like. (According to CM McMillan, "The needs of a future
education system for the RSA," 1989.)

According to The Transvaal Educational News, 87(4),
April 1989, Australia has about 60 000 professional engin-

eers, while in South Africa we have about 15 000. "Australia plans to produce about 40 000 graduate engineers in the next ten years, an average of 4 000 per annum. In South Africa, only about 1 200 engineering graduates are produced per annum. And yet, our population is double Australia's albeit with a significantly smaller GNP."

According to Eskom's John Maree, in 1988 there were 38 000 unemployed matriculants, and this in an era of a desperate skills shortage (see "Get going, Stoffel!" *Financial Mail*, January 26, 1990). It is forecast that South Africa will be facing a major new education crisis in the year 2000 — with the numbers of unemployable, unemployed, and uneducated people rising fast. Statistics indicate that approximately 80% of all white South Africans follow academically oriented courses at school, whilst only 20% decide on career oriented courses. Apparently the figure is even higher in black schools.

❏ The inadequacy of the home environment. It is estimated that 68% of black adults are illiterate and innumerate. These illiterate adults clearly cannot provide a rich learning background for their children.

❏ The educational neglect of generations of non-white pupils. This is a major reason for today's serious social and economic problems. Dr. Renate Lippert, Director of the Centre for Computer-based Instruction at the University of Pretoria, divides the crisis into two categories:

(i) a crisis of quality (which include the relevance of the curricula, teacher training, equal standards for all race groups, the consideration of various cultural values and languages, etc.)

(ii) a crisis of quantity or adequacy (of such factors as funds, schools, teachers, and facilities).

Challenges ahead

According to Dr S Engelbrecht, Executive director: Institute for Educational Research: Human Sciences Research Council

(HSRC), these are some of the most important educational issues for which no solutions have been found:

❑ The phenomenal growth of the black population, which gives rise to rapid growth in the number of primary, secondary, and tertiary learners (Table 7.1). Population growth and demographic trends have an extremely strong influence on the total provision of education.

		WHITE	COLOURED	INDIAN	BLACK	TOTAL
1960	Primary	462	276	111	1 452	2 301
	Secondary	246	29	17	48	340
	TOTAL	708	305	128	1 500	2 641
1980	Primary	608	618	150	4 067	5 443
	Secondary	348	141	67	774	1 330
	TOTAL	956	813	234	6 645	8 646
1987	Primary	547	597	142	5 171	6 458
	Secondary	407	216	91	1 474	2 188
	TOTAL	954	813	234	6 645	8 646
2000	Primary	532 (6 638)	527 (7 842)	137	6 226	7 430
	Secondary	342 (3 191)	320 (3 961)	91	2 453	3 223
	TOTAL	874 (9 829)	847 (11 803)	228	8 679	10 653
2020	Primary	541 (9 109)	472 (10 274)	143	8 082	9 247
	Secondary	358 (5 868)	306 (6 624)	85	4 319	5 075
	TOTAL	899	778	228	12 401	14 322

Table 7.1

NUMBER OF PUPILS IN PRIMARY
AND SECONDARY EDUCATION (1 000s)

Source: Dostal, E., *Notebook on Educational Trends and Perspectives.*
Institute for Futures Research, University of Stellenbosch, 1988.

❑ A relevant school curriculum for all pupils, with consideration for the country's socio-political, economic, and manpower demands.

❑ A credible and acceptable school management and administration system.

❑ The financing of an education system which is steadily becoming unaffordable.

The demands

The demands made by society can only be understood if they're viewed against the background of the present education system. Education and training have become issues of great concern; they also present some of the most critical challenges facing South Africa. These demands are, however, part of the reality of South Africa.

Career education, alternative education, people's education, early childhood education, non-formal education, equal education, distance education, training, and in-service training have all become buzzwords.

The degree to which blacks' educational demands have become politicised is clear from the words of Sebolelo Mohajane, Executive Director of Careers Centre in Soweto and Chairman of the Soweto Parents' Crisis Committee (1986:4): "The student revolts of 1976 and the school boycotts of 1980 heightened certain characteristics of student action that were to become an integral part of the 1980's student's rejection of the State education system. The inadequacies of the State's racist educational system were seen as short-term demands, while the national struggle for liberation — and therefore the linkage to broader community and political issues became an important part of the students' educational struggle."

Socio-economic demands

As I have already pointed out, the educational crisis cannot be viewed in isolation from socio-economic conditions. As Van den Aardweg (1987:174–181) points out:

"The primary causes can be found in the practice of a nation which allows overcrowding, poverty and unemployment and nurtures feelings of isolation, powerlessness and frustration. Prolonged exclusion of any group from a nation's life and from decision making processes which directly affect a group, culminating in feelings of not belonging, have been found to be primary to unrest and violence."

In a paper entitled "Education in the RSA: Realities and Prospects/Compromises," Dr S Engelbrecht, Executive Director: Institute for Educational Research at the HSRC distinguishes between the following demands which are driven by society:

1. SEGREGATED EDUCATION

A large proportion of the white population advocates segregated education, while a strong contingent of blacks, coloureds, and Indians support integrated or desegregated education.

The greatest complaint regarding segregated education is that it is unequal; it is believed that it is intended to be inferior so as to keep blacks in a subordinate position. The "undeniable reality" of the multicultural nature of the South African society is one of the major arguments for segregated education.

2. INTEGRATED EDUCATION

The majority of blacks, coloureds, and Indians will support a fully integrated educational system. Many believe that an integrated system will alleviate the inequalities of the segregated system.

Sebolelo Mohajane (1986) stated in the IPB Journal (5[5], p. 8) that dissatisfaction with black education is a result of apartheid "and all its pillars, i.e. separate education, Group Areas Act, African Homelands, as well as separate voters' rolls. Unless all the above are done away with, there will be no peace."

Coloureds and Indians have taken advantage of the opportunity to open the schools of their two departments to all pupils, subject to certain conditions. However, the following factors would militate against the establishment in the immediate future of a totally integrated school system in South Africa:

❑ Language problems, especially in the lower standards and in rural areas
❑ Differences in school readiness and in levels of cognitive development
❑ Teachers who are not trained to cope with various languages, cultures, religions, and learning needs
❑ Resistance to compulsory integration.

Dr Engelbrecht suggests that establishing a new education department would help deal with much of the present dissatisfaction, and put South Africa on the road to a democratic education system. This department should function independently and provide for "open" (integrated) schools. It could expand as demand increased.

In an article on the "The limits of pluralism," Thomas (1981: 589–591) says that multi-cultural education does not provide all the answers in a heterogeneous population. As he puts it: "Demand to serve the needs of everyone made it almost impossible to serve the needs of anyone." And he goes on to say: "Pluralism leads at its worst to no ethics and at its best to a school with ambivalent ethics of conflict and conformation."

3. PEOPLE'S EDUCATION (ALTERNATIVE EDUCATION)

Blacks' educational demands have shifted from equal education through integrated education towards "people's education" (which is defined as education suited to the needs of today's black person).

The exact meaning of people's education is not clear, but it clearly implies authority over the content and management of education. It is also seen as a political instrument of reform. Arguments for people's education result from both the general political unrest in the country and the specific educational crisis.

Dr. Engelbrecht characterises people's education as follows:

❑ In the hands of the people for whom it is intended
❑ Intended for all, not just for students
❑ Education for literacy as well as for political responsibility
❑ In the interests of the people — relevant to work
❑ Having definite curricular implications.

The government is aware of the revolutionary element implied by people's education. But note has been taken of its positive aspects — for example, that education should be relevant to the needs of people in terms of their aspirations and history.

4. COMPULSORY, UNIVERSAL AND FREE EDUCATION

Blacks have, from earliest times, demanded compulsory education, i.e., education that is universal and free, as it is for whites.

Black education has for years received less pro-rata support from the state than has white education. Black education is seen as inferior and discriminatory.

The consensus view is that black education should be raised to the same level as that of the whites as soon as the economy of the country can afford it. There has also been a movement away from a philosophy of separate education towards the view that a common education curriculum is needed for all.

5. EQUAL EDUCATIONAL OPPORTUNITIES

Demands for equal educational opportunities include free education, compulsory education, and integrated education, as well as people's education. There should also be parity, equality, equity, and the abolition of social inequalities within the educational system.

Blacks' demands for equal educational opportunities include: compensatory and remedial education; equal opportunities for progression; equal career opportunities and access to the professional world; socio-economic and political equalisation; compulsory and free education; and integrated education at all levels.

6. MULTICULTURAL EDUCATION

According to Dr Engelbrecht, multicultural education is not equated to desegregated or integrated education, and it can develop in four ways:

1. Assimilation (capitulation to another culture)
2. Cultural pluralism (acceptance of differences)
3. Total independence (apartheid)
4. Militant action (taking over power from the majority).

While the rest of the world is reacting against an educational policy of assimilation or equalisation, exactly the opposite is happening in South Africa. Here, there is a reaction against a policy of pluralism.

There's an increasing demand that more should be done — even within the present segregated education system — to promote inter-group knowledge and understanding. This demand has implications for guidance, the training of teachers, and so on.

7. RELEVANT EDUCATION

The demand by society for relevant education refers to various deficiencies in the present system, especially as regards to career education.

The core issue is the demand for relevant trained manpower, and education which is geared to technological and economic development.

The uniform provision of facilities

It is generally agreed that every South African must enjoy equal educational facilities, including, for example, libraries and laboratories. Text books must be objective and universal for all groups.

Other factors

In addition to the factors already mentioned, the following issues impact seriously on the quality of education:

❑ Black schools are exponents of the western scientific ideal
❑ Poorly trained teachers aggravate the problem of relevance
❑ White teachers in black schools cannot understand the unique situation of black children
❑ Incongruity between the ideals of the school and those of the home
❑ Increasing incongruity between the cultural environment of the school and that of the home
❑ The western school format is unfamiliar to black pupils.

While the search continues for a better educational dispensation, research indicates that technology can assist in alleviating some of these problems and meeting the challenges facing education in South Africa.

The role of technology

In the view of Business Futures 1987, published by the Institute for Futures Research at the University of Stellenbosch:

"It seems evident that South Africa's educational problems are not likely to be solved by means of the traditional remedies of spending more money, building more schools and training more teachers. It seems unlikely that even large investments in the traditional system could significantly improve the existing situation . . . hence rather bold and imaginative solutions, such as the use of information technologies, will have to be implemented."

A wide variety of technologies are available. Some are especially suited to First World conditions. In a Third World environment, problems arise with the operation of sophisticated equipment and the maintenance of such equipment in rural areas. We should be careful of indiscriminate expenditure on technology in the hope that "gadgets" will solve our educational crisis.

Clearly, technology cannot provide all the answers, but there is certainly no solution without it. It is important that teachers and educators believe technology will assist them in their jobs rather than threaten them.

Educational radio and television

South Africa faces enormous challenges in education. Electronic media have a strategic role to play by supplementing or complementing other methods. However, the successful use of such media demands careful planning, production, selection, and integration.

Television and radio have become common teaching aids for distance education. Both offer their advantages and disadvantages.

For one thing, they are one-way media. Learners cannot interrupt. Secondly, broadcasts occur in "real time," which may be inconvenient for students. And, of course, there's the high cost of television, and the fact that 82% of schools in South Africa don't have mains electricity.

Radio is the most accessible medium of all and is relatively cheap. As Crissel (1986:12) points out, it's virtually the only medium that allows the audience to do other things while using it. Unlike television, radio can operate off batteries, so mains electricity is not necessary.

In 1964, a partnership was established between the Department of Education and Training and the SABC for the production and broadcasting of formal school radio lessons. Informal and non-formal educational programmes have been broadcast on both radio and television since 1984.

Since then, television programmes from foreign sources — for example, Open University and Teleschool — have been broadcast during educational time slots.

Emphasis is placed on locally-produced programmes for pre-schoolers, to prepare them for formal schooling. These programmes are broadcast on radio in five black languages, and on television in English.

An educational breakthrough

In October 1990, the SABC began experimenting with weekday television broadcasts of formal educational programmes for matric pupils. Despite short notice, and despite the lack of time to publish workbooks and back-up materials, feedback from various communities indicated that the effort was a huge success. The total cost of approximately R1 million was largely carried by sponsors.

A great deal of experience was gained in this breakthrough project. Starting early in 1991, the SABC hopes to use spare capacity on its television schedule to broadcast regular educational programmes to schools. Subjects will include mathematics, science, biology, and English. The SABC is cooperating with a number of education departments and educational organisations to make this venture a success.

Early in 1990, Eduspectrum, a highly successful full-day programme which offers vocational guidance, was broadcast on TV1/2/3. Many sponsors were also involved in this programme.

It is of utmost importance to make full use of a multimedia approach in educational broadcasting. Publications such as workbooks are necessary adjuncts to either radio or television, to reinforce facts. Cooperation of the newspapers in offering "hard copy" back-up is essential.

The SABC is one of the most powerful communications media in Southern Africa. So it's important it should be used to its full capacity to supply meaningful educational opportunities for the whole population. The cost of programmes must, however, be borne by educational departments or sponsors, and not by SABC licence holders.

The limitations of video

Video has become an extremely popular medium in education and training. It's relatively cheap and compact, and easily used by both teacher and student. However, videotapes are linear and force students through a predetermined sequence.

Interactive video (IV) was developed to allow rapid access to any of a large number of pictures. Up to 6 000 video images are printed on a special optical videodisc that looks like a large long-playing record. A special videodisc player is hooked to a computer and allows a programmable interaction between user and image. This form of video is expensive, so it's not economically viable in South Africa and few schools can use it. Its application is thus limited and specialised.

One organisation that does make use of interactive video is South African Airways. The technology is appropriate to their needs, and offers highly individualised instruction in audio and video format. Anything from interpersonal to technical skills can be taught this way.

Flexi-learning

In tertiary education especially, there is an increasing need for student flexibility.

According to Dr. Renate Lippert, there is already "a steady increase in the so-called external degree programmes, which permit students, through programmed self-study, testing and work experience, to earn a degree with a minimum of time spent on a campus or in the traditional lecture room." This option is particularly suitable at secondary and even tertiary educational level.

Britain's Open University is probably the best known example, but local examples include UNISA, Vista University, Technikon RSA, and some correspondence schools. According to Dr. Lippert, most "correspondence" and study material will in future be replaced by audio, visual, or computerised formats — i.e., technology will supplement and aid education.

Students will be able to link into computer networks or tune into university radio and television channels. This implies bringing the university to a place convenient to the student, rather than bringing the student to a location convenient to the university. However, I don't believe that this is the answer for the mass education of school pupils.

Community Learning Centres (CLC's)

In a position paper on privatisation, Syncom researcher Andre Spier predicts that economic limitations will force South Africa to a learner-centred education system and that community learning centres (CLC's) will eventually replace schools as we know them today.

According to Spier, the centres "will accommodate preschool headstart programmes, formal foundation courses, continued education programmes, and socio-cultural community programmes.

"This intensive utilisation will warrant the application of the most appropriate and varied teaching technology and data resources. CLC's can be electronically linked to centres of advanced and specialised learning. They will enable users to study any community problem and contribute to its solution.

"An important aspect of electronic linkage is that it will reduce, if not eliminate, qualitative differences between the centres."

CLC's would promote inquiry, creativity, social communication, and problem solving.

Overall cost reduction

The introduction of new technology in education will cost more initially, but in Spier's view, the overall cost of schooling will then fall. Some of the reasons:

❏ Higher teacher:student ratios (up to 1:200)
❏ Use of these technologies by others, not only by formal students
❏ A reduction in the length of formal schooling by up to 50%.

Computer-based education/training

The educational technology that's currently getting most attention is the computer.

During the last 25 years, computers have been proved to significantly reduce learning time, to improve students' performance, and to motivate them. Both the University of the Western

Cape and Rhodes University successfully use computer-based education (CBE).

In primary as well as secondary schools throughout the country, teachers and parents can choose from a large variety of computers and programmes. The National Film Library plays an important role as disseminator of educational software. Dr. Lippert says that CBE is useful for these reasons:

❏ Conventional methods are often inadequate due to the low level of literacy, the shortage of skilled trainers, and conceptual problems experienced by trainers who haven't had adequate formal schooling.

❏ The real environment, as an ideal learning situation in which to learn a skill, is often unavailable or unsuitable due to cost, distance, safety, noise, size, etc.

❏ CBE offers training improvement in terms of consistency, permanence, and quality. Students work in a climate where failure can be tolerated. They get relevant, accurate, and acceptable feedback, as well as the opportunity to evaluate their own performance and to progress at their own pace.

Many major financial institutions develop their own in-house computer-based training. Other companies contract CBE specialists to develop specific training software for them.

Converging technologies

During the past four or five years, says Jacques Hugo of Infoplan, "there has been a convergence of technologies from the entertainment industry, communications, artificial intelligence, data processing, and even the optics industry. This has a revolutionary impact on education and training."

(A negative effect, unfortunately, has been the inadequate exploitation of opportunities created by the technology in South Africa.)

Hugo suggests that the following questions be asked in determining the cost-effectiveness of CBE:

❑ What is the total cost of conventional training vs. the cost of CBE, and what is the value of the training presented by each method?

❑ Is there an improvement in effectiveness and productivity among students?

❑ Is there an increase in the number of students who can be handled by CBE, and can subsistence and travel costs be cut as in the case of conventional courses?

❑ Is there better control over training resources?

❑ Is it easier to standardise course content and presentation?

CBE cannot solve all training and education problems. But it could play an important role in alleviating the country's shortage of technical manpower needs. It can cost-effectively accelerate learning and raise standards; and it gives "the teacher more time to develop more satisfactory training which will enable people to learn to be more independent and have more control over what they learn."

South Africa might not have all the money or manpower resources of a country such as the USA, for example, but as Dr. Lippert points out, we "can compete favourably when it comes to the state-of-the-art in educational technology."

She explains that "on the horizon are technologies which combine audio, text, graphics and full motion video in one medium — the so-called 'hypermedia.' Considerations like storage space and access speed have favoured optical media, like the CD's. . . ." (The CD-1 disk, for example, has a 650 MB storage capacity, and offers 72 minutes of motion video, 6 000 full-frame full-colour images, and 17 hours of audio. Soon, most computers will have drives that can read such disks.)

Time to get our priorities straight

The crisis in South African education will make technology increasingly important in any future educational system. Clearly, if South Africa is to survive economically and politically, something urgently has to be done.

The question is not whether we can afford the necessary steps, but rather, whether we can afford *not* to take them. As Dr. Lippert so rightly says, "only through the multiplier effect of electronics and telecommunications do we have the technology to reach and to instruct vast sections of the population that otherwise would be denied the privileges of education."

In Taiwan and Singapore, illiteracy has virtually vanished and the unemployment problem has virtually been solved as a result of bold national strategies to use radio, television, and computers to uplift the educational standards of the masses.

In Britain, the USA, and Thailand, the Open University and the National Technological University operate via satellite to reach students who are either in remote rural areas or busy earning a living. This is an example to South Africa of how it's possible to provide every citizen with appropriate and interesting education.

But as Professor Mehl of the University of the Western Cape warns, until it becomes a national priority for us to understand the learning needs of the disadvantaged, and how to address them, the use of technologies will remain "shots in the dark."

That said, we would do well to reflect on this quotation from Benjamin Disraeli: "Upon the education of the people of this country, the fate of this country depends".

Acknowledgments

The author wishes to extend a sincere word of thanks to Mr Willie Visagie and his colleagues at the SABC for research and valuable assistance in preparing this paper. A special word of thanks to Dr. Renate Lippert, Director: Centre for Computer-based Instruction, University of Pretoria, and to Dr S.W.H. Engelbrecht, Executive Director: Institute for Educational Research, HSRC.

Chapter Eight

TECHNOLOGICAL ISOLATION AND ILLITERACY

INFERIORITY COMPLEX OR REALITY?

DR GEOFF GARRETT

Dr Geoff Garrett is Executive Vice-President:
Operations at the CSIR (formerly the Council for
Scientific and Industrial Research). A graduate of
Cambridge University, he has studied and worked
at universities in the United States and Canada. He
was Visiting Professor at the University of
Sheffield and head of the Department of
Metallurgy and Materials Engineering at the
University of the Witwatersrand. He has over 80
publications to his credit and is editor of three
books on the fracture of materials. He joined the
CSIR in 1986, and is currently responsible for
operating divisions in the fields of aeronautics,
building, computing, energy, materials,
microelectronics and communications technology,
and production technology.

In considering the role of technology in the changing South Africa, we need first to understand why it is important. We need also to ask what will make us a "winning nation." And we need to examine the international environment — where we're competing, how we are performing, and the nature of change.

Is technology a good investment?

The first issue is the economic impact of technology. Is it a good investment?

Studies by the Office of Technology Assessment of the United States Congress have shown that R&D expenditure yields big returns: financial returns in excess of 20% per year, and social returns in excess of 40%. An estimated seven-eighths of economic growth is attributable to technological change in the broadest sense (including better education of the workforce). Other studies indicate that somewhere between 40% to 90% of a country's economic growth has its origins in technological advances or innovation-related factors.

The second issue to consider is the *speed* of technological advance. We are in a period of intense technology change where, with the globalisation of world markets, increasing and aggressive competition has become the norm. Most of the technologies underlying products that will be on the market by the year 2000 are either already in the laboratories or just entering them. Over the next 12 years it has been estimated that we'll see at least ten times as much technological progress as in the last 12 years. By the end of 1991, for example, the average American automobile will have more on-board computing power than the Apollo spacecraft took to the moon in 1969. That's how far and how fast things have moved in just the past 20 years.

This is also a time of multidisciplinary action on the technology scene. We're breaking down the traditional barriers between the various scientific and technological disciplines. The rate of change is astonishing.

This quote sums up the way many of us may feel:

"The world is too big for us, there is too much doing, too many crimes, casualties, violence and excitement. Try as you will, you get behind in the race in spite of yourself. It's an incessant strain to keep pace and still you lose ground. Science empties its discoveries on you so fast that you stagger beneath them in hopeless bewilderment. The political world witnesses new scenes so rapidly that you're out of breath trying to keep up with them. Everything is high pressure, human nature cannot endure much more".

These words could have been spoken today. In fact, they come from the *Atlantic Journal* of 1837 — over 150 years ago! So change is not something new. It's always been with us.

Just how well is South Africa doing?

As we move into the 1990s, and as the world becomes increasingly dependent on technology, and increasingly comfortable with technological change, we need to take a hard, realistic look at South Africa's potential in the field of technology.

First, let's examine the issue of our technological literacy — or illiteracy. The "three P's" we can use as a rough measure in this area are people, patents, and papers.

We must also look at our relative spending on research and development in the context of the global "playing field." Finally, we must address some education issues, the impact of technology on policy, and some of the challenges ahead of us.

Scientific literacy

The formal definition of scientific literacy says that one should have a minimum understanding of scientific terms, of how science functions, and of the impact of science on society. Taking those three criteria together, fewer than 6% of Americans might be considered scientifically literate. The formal definition is thus of little help in gauging where we stand as a nation, so we need to find other measures.

Let's first try to put South Africa into context. We're an average country with an average economy. We have about 1/200 of the world's GNP, which puts us in line with countries like Yugoslavia, Mexico, Malaysia, Chile, and Brazil. The world as a whole averages about 23 000 scientists and engineers per million of population.The United States has about 126 000. South Africa is way down the scale with only 16 500. This puts us well ahead of the so-called developing countries (with an average 8 000) but still fairly low in this particular league.

Another relevant measure is the number of first degrees in science and engineering per 10 000 of population. Once again, compared with the major industrialised nations, we're a long way down the list, averaging one per 10 000, compared with 47 in the UK, 68 in Japan, and 75 in the USA.

A third measure is the number of scientific articles that our scientists and researchers publish. Here, interestingly enough, we're significantly ahead of Taiwan, Hong Kong, South Korea, and Singapore — the newly industrialised countries (NIC's) that we like to compare ourselves with. We're also significantly ahead in terms of patents, except in comparison to Taiwan (Figure 8.1). So, where this measure of the productivity of our scientific and technological community is concerned, we're actually quite impressive. However, as far as the corresponding impact of science and technology goes, even the most straightforward of economic comparisons would surely beg the question as to how effectively science and technology are being put to work for the benefit of our country and its people.

The total amount of money spent on R&D in South Africa each year amounts to about 0,7% of our GDP, a modest investment in world terms. This is substantially less than *individual firms* spend in the USA, West Germany, or Japan. In fact, as shown in Figure 8.2, the top-spending 30 companies in the world each invest more on R&D than we do as a nation.

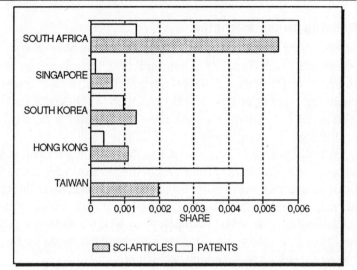

Figure 8.1

SCIENTIFIC AND TECHNOLOGICAL WORLD SHARE
OF SOUTH AFRICA AND ASIAN NIC's (1986–88)

USA

General Motors	$4,75	Digital Equipment	$1,31
IBM	$4,42	General Electric	$1,16
Ford	$2,93	Eastman Kodak	$1,15
AT & T	$2,57	Hewlett Packard	$1,02
Du Pont	$1,32	United Technologies	$0,93

Europe

Siemens (Germany)	$3,68	Hoechst (Germany)	$1,38
Daimler Benz (Germany)	$2,93	ABB (Switzerland)	$1,36
Philips (Netherlands)	$2,15	Fiat (Italy)	$1,24
CGE (France)	$1,81	Ciba-Geigy (Switzerland)	$1,23
Bayer (Germany)	$1,40	Volkswagen (Germany)	$1,20

Japan

Hitachi	$2,19	NTT	$1,52
Matsushita Elect.	$2,14	Toshiba	$1,46
Toyota	$1,90	Nissan	$1,36
NEC	$1,78	Honda	$1,13
Fujitsu	$1,74	Sony	$1,01

SA's total in 1989 is estimated to be R1,8 billion or approximately $0,72 billion.

Figure 8.2

SOUTH AFRICA'S R&D EXPENDITURE RELATIVE TO MAJOR
WORLD COMPANIES (IN BILLIONS OF DOLLARS)
Source: "Innovation" — Special *Business Week* issue, June 1990

Building on our strengths

South Africa is really very accomplished in a number of areas. According to the "Index of Scientific Power," developed by the Foundation for Research Development (FRD), which grades countries in terms of their scientific output, South Africa ranks 21st out of 154 nations. But look at the fields in which we excel: ornithology, ecology, and medicine (Figure 8.3).

It's all very well being a leader in these disciplines, but it's excellence in the "hard" disciplines of the physical sciences and engineering that will really make the difference in terms of economic growth. We currently spend over 40% of our total R&D funds on the social sciences; most western nations spend less than 12%. Being world class bird watchers might be fun, but will it solve our economic problems?

Of course, compared to the rest of Africa, we're a very powerful source of science and engineering talent and ideas. For example, in 1986 (the latest year for which UNESCO figures are

No	FIELD	COUNTRY RANKING
1	Ornithology	4
2	Water Resources	5
3	General & Internal Medicine	7
4	Ecology	8
5	Zoology	10
6	Anaesthesiology	12
7	Metallurgy	13
8	Dentistry	14
9	Geology	14
10	Marine	15
11	Oceanography	16
12	Astronomy	17
13	Respiratory	17
14	Haematology	18
15	Cardiovascular	19
16	Gastroenterology	19
17	Obstetrics	19

Figure 8.3
TOP SOUTH AFRICAN DISCIPLINES

available), South Africa produced 5 794 bachelor-level graduates and 2 561 post-graduates in natural science and engineering. The combined totals for Botswana, Malawi, Mozambique, Swaziland, and Zimbabwe were 247 and 31, respectively. In 1988 South Africa contributed some 44% of all scientific articles from Africa (the other major contributors being Egypt and Nigeria).

Our education handicap

One of our great handicaps is our education system. It's a sad fact that, if we take 1989 as a typical year, not one black student passed the higher grade matric examination with an "A" in maths and science. Comparatively, the number of white students runs into the hundreds.

And that's not the end of the story. Sure, we're pushing some black children through the education system, but what is the quality of that experience? One senior science examiner recently admitted that the problem is severe: "The teachers can't teach and the syllabi bore the kids to sleep." Where the emphasis is on rote learning and not on discovery, the excitement of science and technology is surely missing.

The consequences are predictable. Very few blacks, coloureds, or Asians choose science or technology as a career. So very few enter university to study in these areas, the dropout rate is terrible, and pitifully few graduate. What's more, the blacks who do make it usually take far longer than whites to get their degrees.

You might ask: "How has this happened?" There are of course many reasons and it is dangerous to be simplistic. But what it all comes down to is official policy. For the past 40 years and longer, we have pursued a course which was guaranteed to lead to our failure. The consequences are predictable when Verwoerd, as a future prime minister, could ask in June 1954: "What is the use of teaching a Bantu child mathematics?"

The chairman of the Technology Committee of the South African Chamber of Business (SACOB) said recently that about

32% of the South African workforce is unskilled, compared with 17% in Western Europe. And projections to the year 2000, which show close to 60% of the workforce being unskilled, surely sound a clear warning.

There is general agreement that we need far more people to learn basic trades. But statistics for apprentice registration are alarming — only about 0,7% of the workforce is involved, according to recent Steel and Engineering Industries Federation of South Africa (SEIFSA) figures. Even those systems and facilities that are available to upgrade the general level of skills are thus not being adequately used.

Another concern is the lack of an engineering orientation in tertiary education. We have good universities that teach engineering and we have technikons and technical colleges that teach technical and engineering-related subjects, but their output is extremely small. Thus, SACOB studies show that from 1980–1988 only 4% of university graduates were engineers. Of even greater concern is the fact that only 15% of technikon students were involved with engineering-related courses, while just 20% of students at technical colleges were studying the engineering-related subjects we so badly need.

Are we really technologically isolated?

It would be very easy to blame South Africa's isolation, particularly over the last few years, for all our problems in the field of science and technology. We could argue that politics has done it all, that sanctions have had an overriding impact. But what are the facts? How has our relative isolation affected our technological activity?

Three indicators can help us sort fact from fiction:

1. The current level of scientific and technical cooperation, as indexed by jointly-authored publications across international boundaries
2. The amount of "technology trading" that goes on
3. The flow of scientifically-trained people, particularly during the last decade when so many advances occurred.

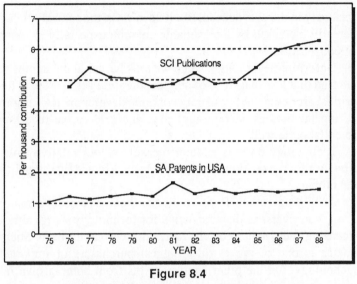

Figure 8.4

SOUTH AFRICA'S CONTRIBUTION TO S&T

First, let's look at South Africa's contribution to international science and technology.

Our scientists account for about six in every 1 000 contributions to referenced international publications, and their output has been moving up quite reasonably (Figure 8.4).

In terms of patents, we're definitely on the low side. But at least we're not falling further behind, in a rapidly expanding technological environment.

A more useful test would be a "cooperation index" which asks: "How much cooperation is there through formal publications in science and technology between South Africa and the rest of the world?" If we compare our performance with the 36 most productive countries ranked this way, South Africa is near the bottom. However, we're in pretty good company (Japan is below us!) so this factor probably doesn't have a major impact.

If we look in detail at this measure of cooperation (namely at the number of scientists cited as co-authors of books and articles in major journals), we might expect it to have declined seriously in the past decade. But it hasn't. On the contrary, it has actually increased by a reasonable amount, especially in terms of cooperation with the US.

Unfortunately, though, when we look harder at the numbers, we find that less than 10% of our "cooperation activity" is in the critical areas that underpin our economic development — engineering, technology, and the applied sciences. Here, we're failing to collaborate well.

Technology trade is another measure of our relative isolation, or otherwise. How much has it been affected by the political climate?

According to the Reserve Bank, there has been a major growth in overseas disbursements for technology — royalties, licensing fees, and so on. In fact, on a per capita basis South Africa is one of the world's biggest purchasers of imported technology. On the other hand, receipts from home-grown inventions are relatively modest (Figure 8.5).

If we plot the results as a "technology balance of payments ratio" — technology in vs. technology out — we're once again near the bottom of the league table. Surprisingly, we don't do too well when compared with many of the countries we might view as less technologically developed than ourselves (Figure 8.6).

Another interesting indicator is the relative growth in R&D expenditure, first by local firms, and then by foreign-owned firms in South Africa. And here's another surprise: at the very peak of disinvestment, foreign firms substantially *increased* their local R&D spending relative to South African firms. One might conclude that they were simply hedging their bets, protecting themselves against the possible impact of disinvestment, but the fact is, they invested a good deal of money here. In contrast, a developing culture in local industry of "not invented here, so it must be better," supporting our huge bill for imported technology, undermines efforts to establish local centres of internationally competitive excellence.

A third issue is immigration and emigration, particularly of technically-trained professionals. The official statistics don't

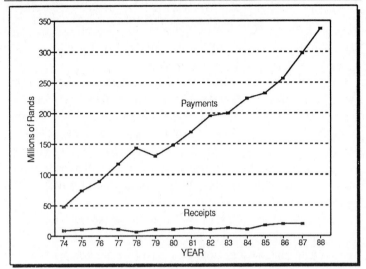

Figure 8.5

ROYALTIES, COPYRIGHTS AND PATENTS

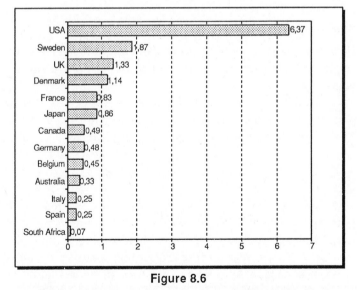

Figure 8.6

TECHNOLOGICAL "BALANCE OF PAYMENTS" RATIO

look too bad, but they don't tell the whole story. Of real concern is the number of people who have gone on extended holidays or educational leave, and never returned.

Official figures say that fewer than 2 000 people emigrated each year in the past few years. But more realistic estimates by the Scientometric Advisory Service of the FRD put the number as high as 12 000 a year — and obviously a good number of those would be highly qualified scientists and engineers. Equally, it has become more and more difficult to recruit people from overseas. The tap has been virtually turned off, as the CSIR's own statistics clearly show: overseas recruitment dropped from close to 100 in 1982 to almost zero five years later. Our local environment has become distinctly unattractive, but we really need those additional skills. A loss of person-to-person contact and the injection of new skills from abroad has also led to a "we can do it on our own" mind-set, dangerous beyond measure as the world moves towards a "global village."

The bottom line

How do these overlapping aspects of our technological illiteracy and isolation impact on our performance as a nation? What's the bottom line?

If we review a few key indicators, the future is rather depressing. Unemployment has risen from 25% in 1960 to at least 35% — and possibly much higher — in 1990. Real GDP per capita, corrected for inflation, hasn't grown at all. Our share of world exports was cut in half between 1980 and 1989, from 1,3% to 0,6%.

Many say that manufacturing must be our saviour in the years ahead. Gavin Relly, former chairman of Anglo American, said about five years ago: "It's only by doubling our manufacturing base by the year 2000 and remaining competitive enough to boost our manufacturing exports, as well as expanding our domestic market, that we can hope to achieve the kind of economic growth which will allow us to meet even the basic aspirations of all South Africans."

But can we actually make that happen? Where will the investment come from? Manufacturing's contribution to the economy over the past 20 years has not been particularly impressive. In fact, it hasn't really changed at all, remaining more or less steady at a little over 20% of our GDP.

The emergence of the global economy means that a nation's competitiveness is now determined not so much by its natural resources as by its ability to generate and deploy new knowledge. In other words, by its ability to add value to the resources which it has been given.

Within this framework, our performance can be summed up by our "technological balance of payments," and particularly by its change over time. Thus, we've been slightly positive in low-tech products (food, beverages, paper, etc.) but poor — and getting worse — in terms of both medium-tech (household appliances, machinery) and high-tech products (microelectronics, aerospace, drugs, and so on). We still rely heavily on costly imports of the more sophisticated products, and are far from getting our act together in the face of increasing global competition (Figure 8.7).

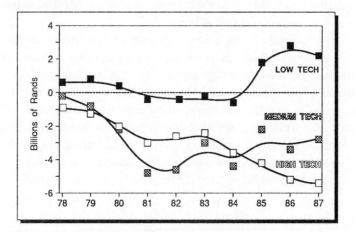

Figure 8.7
SOUTH AFRICAN BALANCE OF PAYMENTS ACCORDING TO
TECHNOLOGICAL INTENSITY

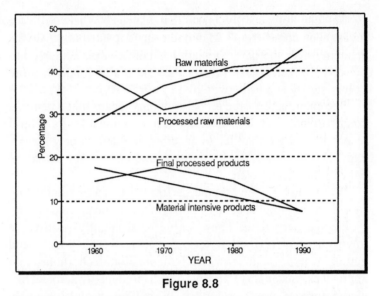

Figure 8.8

EXPORT CATEGORIES AS % OF SOUTH AFRICAN PRODUCTS

Raw materials have accounted for more and more of our exports over the past 30 years, while value-added activities have contributed less and less. In these terms, we're worse off now than we were in 1960 (Figure 8.8).

Our problem is not unique. Various studies show that most resource-rich countries are struggling to develop vibrant, export-driven manufacturing sectors. Most of our competitors in the supply of resources to the world are aggressively researching how to develop their manufacturing industries. All studies and past performance show that the problem is a complex one, requiring in-depth, multi-faceted holistic strategies, rather short-term crisis management approaches. The phrase "resource-rich" has more recently become "resource-cursed."

Lessons for the future

South Africa currently finds itself preoccupied with the process of constitutional negotiation. An important lesson from the world community is that no country has been able to democratise its political structures at a time of negative economic growth. So the goal of sustainable, healthy economic growth is vital to long-term success in the socio-political arena. In an international playing field, and in the face of technology-driven global competition, a solid technological base must surely be critical for our longer-term survival.

As far as our technological literacy is concerned, we do actually have a sound foundation on which to build. As far as our performance in the international business of science and technology goes, our track record is pretty good — particularly if we are realistic about our comparisons.

But there's also no doubt that we have to question our current balance of effort and resource allocation. The physical sciences and engineering are the technological engines for economic growth, and here we're undoubtedly heading for troubled waters.

Over the longer-term, however, if we hope to survive and thrive in a technological world, we simply have to sort out our priorities and focus on first things first, and second things not at all.

"Ordinary" literacy must dominate the agenda. Clem Sunter's portrait of a "winning nation" showed clearly the over-riding importance of quality education, and his South Korean example says it all (Figure 8.9).

With so many calls on talent, time, energy, and money as the new South Africa bursts forth, investment in education, and especially in technology education, is our investment in the future. The yields will be significant, the rewards great. If we make the investment now, South Africa has a real chance over the long haul. If we fail to make it — or if we try to make do with less than sufficient — we will be out of the game forever.

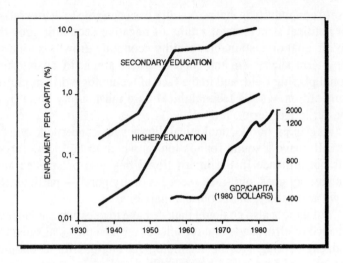

Figure 8.9

EDUCATION — A LEAD INDICATOR
FOR TECHNOLOGICAL "TAKE-OFF"
THE SOUTH KOREAN EXAMPLE

Acknowledgements

Sincere thanks and appreciation are due to the following people for making available some useful facts and figures to help in the development of this chapter: Mr Ted Adlard, SACOB; Dr Brian Clark, CSIR; Dr Chris Garbers; and Dr Anastasios Pouris, FRD.

Chapter Nine
THE GROWING IMPORTANCE OF CROSS-BORDER LIAISON

RUSTY EVANS

Rusty Evans is a Deputy Director-General of the Department of Foreign Affairs. He has spent 25 years as a diplomat in Lisbon, Rio de Janeiro, Sao Paulo, Washington, and London. He was head of the Department's Training Division and Chief Director of the Ministry of Foreign Affairs. Today, he is largely responsible for the direction and coordination of government relations with the rest of Africa, including the development of trade and economic cooperation.

The world is on the threshold of a new era in international affairs. There is no continent on earth in which new relationships and structural changes are not taking place. A new tide has swept away the vestiges of the Cold War, and prior to the Gulf crisis, a climate of growing understanding and trust was being created through dialogue.

The changing world order affects Africa as much as it does Europe and elsewhere. In the regional context, the conflicts in Mozambique and Angola are today seen as relics of a bygone era.

At an international conference a few weeks ago, a Mozambican delegate acknowledged that a new era of bilateral and multilateral contact and cooperation has dawned in Southern Africa. Similar sentiments are being expressed more and more frequently by the spokesmen of frontline states, and within regional organisations such as SADCC and the PTA.

A review of South Africa's relationship with its neighbours, and further afield in Africa, is the subject of intense debate at this time, not least in African capitals.

Realism is shaping relationships

A marked feature of the growing rapprochement between South Africa and both neighbouring and more distant states is a sense of realism. Future regional relations, both political and economic, will evolve through a process which is likely to unfold slowly and progressively.

Consensus is emerging as to the need for closer cooperation and advancement of the mutual interests of the states in the region. This process is influenced by a number of factors. It is taking place against the background of domestic initiatives within South Africa which are directed at creating a new, non-racial and democratic political order in our country.

In the opinion of the United Nations' fact finding mission to South Africa in June 1990, developments in this direction offer real promise for constructive political discussions, and hold encouraging prospects for the dismantling of apartheid. There is a growing recognition of the irreversibility of changes in South Africa's domestic policies. This is influencing African governments to engage in closer dialogue with South Africa.

Six key factors at work in regional affairs

A number of factors affect relations with our neighbouring states, including:

1. Concern about Western Europe's preoccupation with preparations for economic union in 1992.
2. The vast opportunity for trade and investment that has been opened up by the dramatic changes in the USSR and Eastern Europe.
3. Foreign investors and donor nations have become totally disillusioned with Africa's economic and political development. As a result, Africa is becoming marginalised on the international agenda. There is even talk of "de-linkage" from Africa because of the perception that there is simply no hope for the rehabilitation of the continent.
4. There is growing awareness among African leaders that their former western and Soviet-bloc allies are simply losing interest in Africa.
5. We have probably seen the end, for the time being, of superpower competition for influence in Africa. Neither the US nor the Soviet Union has a major interest in Africa today. France is the world power with the most influence on the continent.
6. South Africa's credibility in Africa is growing, boosted by the role we played in the Namibian independence process. Negotiations which led to a series of agreements signed in Brazzaville, Geneva, and New York in 1988, entailed contact with a wide range of African leaders and personalities; scrupulous observance of these agreements has enhanced our credibility in Africa.

Today, South Africa has no quarrel with its neighbours. On the contrary, there are encouraging indications that governments in the region see merit in a regional network of shared assets, resources, and development projects, and from an association with the motor force of the region, South Africa. Creating a framework for cooperation is now the major foreign policy objective of the Department of Foreign Affairs.

Lessons from the past

In 1960, at the height of independence fever in Africa, Kwame Nkrumah reflected: "If we are to remain free, if we are to enjoy the full benefits of Africa's enormous wealth, we must unite to plan for the full exploitation of our human and material resources in the interests of all our people."

Unfortunately, many attempts to form effective regional associations in Africa were doomed to failure. As the Secretary General of the Organisation of African Unity said recently: "Our ancient continent is now on the brink of disaster, hurtling towards the abyss of confrontation, caught in the grip of violence, sinking into the dark night of bloodshed and death."

From a socio-economic perspective, one is torn between despair and hope for the African continent and its 600 million inhabitants. The United Nations Development Programme reports that of all the developing regions of the world, Africa has the lowest life expectancy figures, the highest infant mortality rate, and the lowest literacy rate. There are many barometers that unanimously predict a bleak outlook for the continent in the 1990s.

To put it bluntly, Africa is being left behind. It cannot compete on the economic front with the developed world because of its low technological expertise and administrative incapacity. It has incurred a debilitating external debt of some $250 billion which it cannot begin to service. (This represents 80% of the gross national product of the continent. If one considers that the level for Latin America is 60%, the gravity of the situation is apparent.)

Increasingly, Africa is dependent on foreign aid — some $15 billion in 1990. And it is unable to beneficiate its primary products, the prices of which remain depressed and which continue to be exploited by the developed world.

Yet our continent is endowed with great potential richness. It has abundant natural resources. Southern Africa in particular is a treasure house of valuable strategic minerals. It has more than adequate agricultural resources and the potential to become one of the most prosperous regions of the world.

In the interest of survival, the nations of Southern Africa must join hands and work together. Factors that divided people in our region in the past — colonialism, wars, conflict, and racial strife — are fortunately behind us.

There is a changing mood *within* South Africa, too. There is a growing realisation that true independence and a national identity can only be reached once economic stability has been achieved.

Attaining that stability means there must be peace in South Africa and in Angola and Mozambique. Stability is infectious. Regional stability cannot be divorced from domestic stability in individual states in the region.

Everybody wins

South Africa is the economic power and motor-force in the region. But despite our economic pre-eminence, the benefits of interaction with our neighbouring states are not one-sided.

Existing regional ventures such as the Cahora Bassa hydro electric scheme, the Lesotho Highlands water project, and the Sua Pan Soda Ash project in Botswana — all of which have foreign funding — set a pattern for interaction from which the entire region will benefit. And it can be readily expanded as demands grow in the future.

Such inter-regional interaction entails partnership between independent states. It does not demean any one of them. And it promotes economic development.

Trade with Africa is growing fast

South Africa's total trade with Africa is growing by leaps and bounds. It currently amounts to almost R10 billion a year. Markets are being developed far and wide. Trade with Zaire has trebled in two years. Madagascar has opened up, and there is no reason why trade with that country should not quickly match that with Mauritius — in excess of R300 million per annum. South Africa's non-bank investments in Africa are approximately R4 billion.

During recent overseas visits the Minister of Foreign Affairs, Mr Pik Botha, has presented a development programme for Southern Africa to both western and regional leaders. This programme is based on the premise that there is hope for the ten or 11 states that make up Southern Africa. It is an attempt to harness the promising potential of the region with its large population, developing markets, and abundant natural resources.

South Africa has an excellent infrastructure, good communications, and technology appropriate to the region. But this infrastructure is underutilised.

We see South Africa's contribution to the development of Southern Africa as being mostly in the areas of technology including research and advisory services and the supply of goods and materials. The most important areas, we believe, are:

❏ Agriculture — appropriate techniques of crop and animal husbandry, mechanisation, irrigation and marketing, seed control, plant and animal health, protection against insect and other pests, inland fisheries, agricultural and forest-based industrial activities.

❏ Mining — prospecting, development, production, management, training, living conditions for labour, testing of machinery and equipment.

❏ Building and construction — low-cost housing, road and dam construction, water supply for domestic and agricultural purposes.

❏ Business development — promotion of small-scale industrial and commercial ventures, the creation of marketing facilities, business training.

❏ Human health — organisation of preventative and curative services, family planning, diagnostic services and research.

❏ Education and training — facilities to improve basic skills, the training of artisans, technicians, and medical and veterinary personnel.

❏ Diverse technical fields — transport, telecommunications, the use of fissionable materials, industrial effluent and waste disposal, and environmental protection.

Trade and investment will continue to play a crucial role. South Africa has traditionally supplied its neighbours with building materials, equipment, machinery, pharmaceutical products, agricultural chemicals, and food.

We are convinced in Foreign Affairs that if the region's resources were effectively combined, Southern Africa would be well-placed to compete in a tough world environment, and to claim a rightful share of available aid and development resources.

Our concept of self-help coincides with that expressed at a recent consultative conference of SADCC in Lusaka. We support the view of a SADCC discussion paper presented in Gaborone in August 1990 that "The sole focus will be on the social and economic betterment of the region."

It is essential for the survival of the region that we share resources and present a large, dynamic, and stable market to the world. This would undoubtedly attract investment from abroad, without which Southern Africa cannot survive.

Prospects for peace

South Africa has no interest in the economic debilitation of its neighbours. Our destiny is linked to Africa. We will all be dragged down if economic revival cannot be achieved in this region.

South Africa must persuade its neighbours by its actions that
it is not intent on their destruction. We recognise that we have
to make up lost ground. However, we have seen Namibia to independence. The parties to the conflict in Angola and Mozambique have expressed
confidence in our ability to help bring peace to their countries,
and we are actively involved behind the scenes. Ultimately,
however, the parties concerned have to settle their differences
themselves.

Angola and Mozambique

The prospects for peace in Angola are very good. Both the
MPLA government and the Unita movement have committed
themselves to a peaceful resolution of their conflict. Several
rounds of discussion have already taken place in Lisbon. There
is reason to believe that a cease-fire should be reached by the
end of 1990, and that political reconciliation, which will not be
easy, will bring peace to Angola for the first time in 30 years.

In the case of Mozambique, peace talks have also commenced. Several meetings between the Frelimo government and
Renamo have taken place in Rome, which hold good prospects.
What is even more encouraging is the boldness with which
President Chissano is creating a multi-party democracy and an
open economy in Mozambique.

Getting closer to other African states

We are speaking with many other African governments. Prior to
February 1990 this would have been impossible. I could mention
Madagascar, Kenya, Zambia, and Zimbabwe — even Egypt and
Nigeria, and several more who are still reluctant to publicly
acknowledge contact with South Africa.

The new tide in world affairs has brought a season of political and economic pragmatism to Southern Africa. South Africa
has demonstrated that it is not an enemy of its neighbours, and
should not be seen as one. We will continue to prove this fact.
We have to persuade our neighbours that we're partners in the

development of the sub-continent and that we must all work together to ensure its survival.

Speaking out for the region

Just as Germany, France, and Britain dominate the European economic community, so South Africa is essential to the economic viability of our region.

The economic prosperity generated within the European community has had a positive effect on states on its periphery — Austria, Turkey, and Switzerland (as well as Spain and Portugal, which are the most recent members of the EEC).

Similarly, those countries in South Africa's orbit fared best in terms of gross national product in the 1980s. Botswana, Zimbabwe, Swaziland, Lesotho, and Namibia had noticeably higher GNPs than other African countries. We agree with the assessment of *The Economist* that "The most powerful idea at the end of the 20th Century is the huge advantage of economic togetherness".

But South Africa does not have the financial resources to replace or even supplement the development aid which is so desperately needed in Southern Africa and beyond. So we are engaged in persuading Europe — Western Europe, and the European Community, in particular — to provide the financial backing for close cooperation between the countries of Southern Africa.

To attract development assistance and investment to this region, we advance these compelling reasons:

❏ Southern Africa is a coherent, attractive, and viable economic and commercial entity
❏ The South African economy, together with its technology, management, and skills, is available for the benefit of the development of the region
❏ Coordinated infrastructural development programmes could improve economic prosperity within the countries of the region

❑ There is an existing infrastructural independence in the region which should be better utilised

❑ There is a need for trilateral development projects and investment for the economic benefit of the region.

South Africa's hand of friendship

As democracy is broadened in South Africa, and a new South Africa dawns, we are extending a hand of friendship to Africa.

The future of the sub-continent lies not abroad but in Africa itself. As Europeans have found their destiny in Europe and Americans in the Americas, so South Africans are on the verge of playing their rightful role in Southern Africa and finding our destiny on this continent.

Chapter Ten
THE DEVASTATING IMPACT OF AIDS

DR DENNIS SIFRIS

Dr Dennis Sifris is a general practitioner in private
practice, and head of the HIV Clinic at the
Johannesburg General Hospital. He has been
treating people with HIV infection since 1983. He
is also involved in the development of various
education programmes, including prevention,
effecting behavioral change in different population
groups, testing procedures, patient care, and
infection control.

Only a decade ago, AIDS, or the Acquired Immune Deficiency Syndrome, was completely unknown. It was first identified in 1981. Today no nation on earth can escape its consequences.

The World Health Organisation (WHO) estimates that eight to ten million people in over 150 countries have been infected with the Human Immunodeficiency Virus (HIV), the causative agent of AIDS. Most, if not all of those infected, will develop AIDS and die prematurely. WHO estimates that by the end of this decade, 15 to 20 million people will be infected worldwide.

AIDS has been declared a global pandemic. It has touched almost every aspect of society. Its reach extends to every social institution, including families, schools, communities, businesses, courts of law, the military, the state, and local governments.

The AIDS pandemic has had a profound effect on the way science, medicine, and public health are practised. The social, cultural, political, and economic reaction and response that follows in its wake is an epidemic which will be as important to our future as the virus itself.

The origins of HIV

Reactions to AIDS in South Africa have been extremely varied, ranging from denial and disinterest to apathy and antagonism. Most people are not aware of the threat of AIDS, or they simply choose to ignore it. Everyone agrees that AIDS will cause a tragedy of unprecedented proportions in Southern Africa; however, most people feel it's a problem that affects others, "not me."

Many white South Africans believe that AIDS is a black disease. Some blacks see it as a white racist plot to stop population growth; others don't perceive it as a problem at all. Virtually everybody believes that AIDS is a gay disease.

This element of denial is a major problem in any AIDS programme. Many people, especially those indulging in high-risk behaviours, have implicit faith in medical science; they're encouraged by media reports of an "imminent breakthrough" in finding a cure or a vaccine for AIDS.

Unfortunately, though, a cure or vaccine is a long way off. Even if an effective, inexpensive vaccine were discovered tomorrow, it would be impossible to get it to those who needed it. We have very effective vaccines for diseases such as tuberculosis and measles, yet thousands of people succumb to these diseases.

More has been written about AIDS in this decade than about any other disease, yet still many myths exist about it. Even the origin of the disease is a mystery, and has caused social and political problems.

Many theories have done the rounds — AIDS is "divine retribution," it was manufactured by the CIA or the KGB, and so on. The most widely accepted theory is that HIV is a mutation of a similar virus found in African green monkeys. Mutation is a natural process that constantly occurs in nature; although the first cases of AIDS were recognised in the US, the virus probably mutated to its present form in Central Africa in the 1960s and was identified two years after the first cases occurred.

How the virus is spread

It's important to stress that HIV is not highly contagious. It is not passed on by sweat, saliva, or casual contact. It is not spread through the air or transmitted by insects. It cannot be passed on by food or eating utensils, or in the working environment. (Work place education programmes should stress this, as many people have, from sheer ignorance, refused to share a work station or to accept food prepared by an HIV carrier.)

HIV is transmitted from person to person in only three ways:

1. By intimate sexual contact
2. By injection of blood
3. Transplacentally — i.e., by a pregnant woman to her unborn child.

When a person is infected with HIV, the first sign is the development of antibodies. These are specific to HIV and are easily detected by a simple blood test; they don't destroy the virus.

The virus enters its target cell, the T-Helper cell, and becomes dormant. (T-Helper cells form the basis of the immune response.) This is the so-called "asymptomatic stage" or "carrier stage" of HIV infection, and it can last anywhere from two to 15 years depending on various co-factors.

During this stage, HIV carriers are healthy and can carry on living and working normally. When the virus is activated, symptoms appear. As HIV multiplies it destroys the T-Helper cells. If activation continues unchecked, the number of T-Helper cells decreases and the body's immune system becomes deficient, leaving it prone to certain opportunistic infections. These are rare and unusual, and are called "AIDS defining diseases." When one is diagnosed, the person by definition has AIDS. So AIDS is the end stage of HIV infection.

For each individual with AIDS, there are 50 to 100 with HIV. One problem in correctly assessing the magnitude of the epidemic is that most reporting systems refer to people with AIDS, and there are few reliable studies of the numbers who are HIV-infected. If we're to make any predictions, we must look at the number infected with AIDS as well as the number infected with HIV.

The epidemic would potentially spread from asymptomatic HIV carriers who may be totally unaware of their infectivity — estimated at about eight to ten million people worldwide.

Accurate predictions are difficult. Many researchers have forecast pessimistic "doomsday" scenarios. They warn that entire villages and populations will be wiped out, leaving a trail of devastation. Countries will be socially, politically, and economically crippled.

Indeed, in some parts of central Africa — especially the eastern shores of Lake Victoria and countries like Burundi, Uganda, Rwanda, and even Zaire — it seems that this fantastic prediction has already come true.

On the other hand, the optimists say that AIDS is being blown out of all proportion and that the official Department of Health statistic of only 500 AIDS cases in South Africa cannot be considered a serious epidemic.

The truth probably lies between the two views. But there's no question that AIDS will be a major problem for South Africa in the 1990s. Nor can any industry or company afford to plan for the future without taking AIDS into account.

A conservative forecast

Extensive research and analysis by a major company provides the following picture of AIDS in South Africa.

Some 600 references and 350 data sources were used, including the World Health Organisation, the South African Institute of Medical Research, hospitals and clinics, blood transfusion services, insurance companies and consultants, and international AIDS data bases. Only published and reliable data of epidemiological studies was used; estimates were excluded.

The information was plotted on a logarithmic graph to show the pattern of infection. The classic S-curve which emerged is the accepted pattern of an epidemic disease.

If the data is divided into three groups — Central Africa, Southern or "middle" Africa, and South Africa — there's a progressive decrease in the numbers as we move southwards. This fits with what is known about the AIDS epidemic. The epicentre is in Central Africa and the epidemic has spread along the trucking routes through Africa.

Doubling time of the disease is about 12 months in industrialised countries. In Africa it is 5,5 to ten months, and the pattern will probably be similar in South Africa.

The following assumptions therefore seem reasonable:

```
Doubling time  . . . . . . . . . . . . . . . . .8 months
% of population at risk  . . . . . . . . . . . . . 30%
Population already infected . . . . . . . . . . . 0,5%
Population growth rate  . . . . . . . . . . . . . 2,5%
Sexually active group  . . . . . . . . . . . . 18 to 65
```

Economically active group . . . . 18 to 65
Death rate after infection 100%
Babies surviving HIV parents 50%
Duration of HIV-positive stage . . . . 5 years
Duration of ARC stage . . . . 2 years
Duration of AIDS stage . . . . 2 years
Sexual behaviour change . . . . None before 1996
Effective cure/vaccine . . . . none
Incidence of child abuse . . . . none under 18

The figures indicate a slowdown in the growth of the South African population by 1999 and a decrease from 2000. The population will then continue to decline for the following three to four years to below its present level.

Some people might think this is marvellous, that AIDS is the answer to the universal problem of over-population. They might argue that AIDS could solve many of the problems of the new South Africa.

But this view simply fails to take into account the host of problems that AIDS will trigger. Consider, for example, its impact on productivity.

About 40% of the population is non-productive. People in this group — who include children and the aged — are not at risk. The major impact of AIDS will be in the 18 to 65-year-old group — people who are both sexually and economically active. So any decline in population as a result of AIDS will affect only the productive work force.

If 60% of the work force is at risk, 0,5% are already infected, and the doubling time is eight months, vast numbers of people will become HIV positive within four years. Some will begin to show signs on sickness by then. AIDS deaths will start to occur in about eight years.

By 2000, we'll see a serious reduction in productivity. The workforce will be half as big as it is today — and will have to bear the burden of those who are ill with AIDS.

Consider what this means to a typically labour-intensive South African company. By 2000, only 30% of the original labour force could be left. And this scenario applies to the police force, nursing, and every other industry or organisation. One fact is clear. *AIDS will affect our future.* It would be extremely foolish to plan for the 1990s without taking it into account. If we are in any way.to manage its effects, it is crucial that top management and policy makers are jolted out of their denial.

The economic impact

The economic effects of AIDS have hardly been felt. But the costs mount every time another person becomes affected.

Insurance companies and medical aid schemes have reacted by excluding people with HIV/AIDS. But in the end the real cost of AIDS will be carried by the state and the private sector — in other words, by the man in the street.

The South African government has called on commerce and industry to assist in the campaign against AIDS. So far, this call has gone largely unheeded. I'm personally unaware of any AIDS prevention campaign sponsored by any industry or company.

At a conference in April 1990, the ANC issued a statement on HIV/AIDS in Southern Africa. Among other things, the organisation called for the involvement of senior political figures in AIDS campaigns. A high public profile would undoubtedly raise the awareness of AIDS and stimulate appropriate action. The ANC has criticised the government approach as being "fundamentally limited and flawed," and "not displaying any genuine commitment to dealing with the problem facing the population."

Strategies for business

What should industry and large companies be doing to deal with this disaster?

Every organisation should have an AIDS policy. However, many resist the idea, arguing that:
1. AIDS should be dealt with like any other debilitating disease

2. A policy might commit them to something that is impossible in the future
3. There's still too much uncertainty about the disease and its legal ramifications
4. Written policy may suggest approval of high-risk or morally unacceptable behaviours.

(Adapted from *AIDS: Corporate America Responds*, 1988.)

Here are reasons for a policy on AIDS:

1. It could help keep experienced people at work even though they were infected, thus avoiding hiring or re-training costs
2. It could reduce the possibility of go-slows or walk-outs by co-workers, fearful of infected employees
3. A standardised, countrywide approach would gain employee respect
4. A clearly-stated policy would provide employee support
5. By anticipating problems and being prepared to respond to questions, a crisis could be avoided
6. Employees would be more confident knowing that their employer had thoroughly studied the issue
7. By reviewing health insurance and benefits plans, the costs of AIDS could be controlled
8. Legal problems could be avoided
9. A clear AIDS policy would help promote a company's image as responsible and caring
10. Education programmes would help prevent the spread of AIDS.

(Adapted from Business Leadership Task Force, USA, 1988)

Developing an AIDS policy

The first step in developing a sound AIDS policy is to establish a task force of key personnel, including top management and union representatives. People from such areas as medical, safety, personnel, public relations, legal, and corporate communications should all be involved.

This group should gather as much information as possible about the disease, its effect, and its management. They should review existing personnel policies and practices, and insurance and medical aid plans. Then they should draft a comprehensive proposal, and a budget. AIDS will affect all future planning. The only way to deal with it is through planning.

Any programme should include education to change behaviour and thus to decrease the rapid spread of the disease. Educational efforts should be community-based, and should be sponsored by both individual firms and by industry at large.

Starting right now, there should be some provision for the cost of AIDS in every budget. In the short term, the disease will cause considerable disruption. But those industries and organisations that act now will survive the problem, and will probably end up more prosperous and successful for the effort.

Chapter Eleven
OUR FRAGILE WORLD

DR IAN PLAYER

Dr Ian Player is an internationally-known nature
conservationist. He was the founder of the
Wilderness Leadership School in Natal, and of
similar bodies in other countries. He has delivered
papers at many international conferences and holds
many honours and awards, including the
Decoration for Meritorious Services, the highest
civilian award made by the South African
government. He is widely known for his
development of anti-poaching programmes, his
contribution to the capture and translocation of the
white rhinoceros, and for initiating the
Duzi Canoe Marathon.

I once approached my job in conservation in the light of cold science. I was always seeking a scientific explanation for what I saw and heard — the kind of soil different trees grew in, the aerodynamics of birds, the biological niches of animals. For me, the scientific values of everything were paramount, and I tried to justify the existence of the game reserves in which I worked in terms of their scientific value. I deliberately distanced myself emotionally. I said, "You cannot quantify beauty scientifically".

Well, the scientific method and the contribution of science to nature conservation have been absolutely invaluable. But they haven't stopped the destruction; in fact, in some instances they've actually aided it.

While my head was working on the scientific approach, another part of me had an inner awareness of the earth and the rhythms that were going on all around me. What I had been concentrating on was the body of Africa; I'd been ignoring her soul.

Then in 1954, when I was stationed in the Ndumu Game Reserve on the Mozambique border, someone sent me Laurens van der Post's book *Venture to the Interior*.

I began to read it very early one evening, when the hippo were leaving the Pongola Valley, their long deep grunts echoing in the dusk. I heard the nightjars calling and the Tonga drums beating to keep the elephants away from the crops. Then, after a while, it was only the book and myself and I was totally caught up in the story.

The next thing I knew was the sound of the hippos going back to the river after grazing all night, and the long, drawn-out, lyrical call of the fish eagle; it was morning and sunlight flooded my room.

Africa's soul

Laurens van der Post made me realise that Africa had a soul and that you had to relate to Africa with your heart. And as the years went by and we were very deeply engaged in conservation battles, it was a combination of the heart and the mind that won those battles, with the heart having an edge.

World science is now beginning to accept that there are other forces in our lives.

All my life I have been interested in history. I am descended from an Englishman who came out here in 1850 with the settlers, and who married a young Afrikaans girl who was conceived and born during the Great Trek. The history of Natal and Zululand is in my blood.

If you stand in your room in one of the hotels along Durban's beachfront and you look at that great sweep of the Natal Coast, and if you cast your mind back to 1487, you can imagine the thrill that Vasco da Gama got when he looked out onto this land on that misty Christmas morning. He called it "Natal."

You only have to read the books of Nathaniel Isaacs, of Henry Francis Fynn, and of all the other early settlers, to get a bird's eye view of what Durban bay looked like.

There were hippo, great shoals of fish, clear running rivers. There were crocodiles in the Umgeni, elephants everywhere. There were great concentrations of pelicans, flamingos, ibis, waders, green shank, and sandpipers. At night you heard the lion roaring, a hyena whooping, and the call of the jackal. The earth was vibrant and alive with wild song.

But look around today and what do you see? Civilisation has arrived, and a once beautiful land has been changed beyond recognition.

Cry of the fish eagle

I can clearly remember 1946. I was 19 and just back from Italy, where I'd been serving in the 6th South African Armoured Division. I was walking down West Street early one morning and I heard a fish eagle calling. As it called and the sound echoed about the buildings, a tug blew its horn; and the two sounds melted into each other. I've never forgotten it, because that was the epitome of what civilisation should actually be. Natural wilderness within the city.

In 1946 Durban still had a soul. Now it has been crushed under concrete. It has become like so many other cities of the world. All Holiday Inns are the same, all paddling pools are the same, all fun parks are the same. There are very few cities now that retain a character, an atmosphere. They have lost their souls.

Ever since I entered the conservation field in 1952 it has been my unfortunate fate, and that of many of my colleagues, to stand up frequently against mindless destruction and to try and conserve tiny fragments of this land as it once was.

An English poet, Victoria Sackville-West, wrote a line that contains an eternal truth. She said: "A man and his land make a man and his creed."

The truth of this line is all about us, if we would care to look. It should be the aim of every South African to ensure that the land that is handed down to the next generation in trust is enriched by our devotion to it.

Our rivers are dying

For 40 years, I have been monitoring our rivers in one way or another. In 1950, I pioneered the Umzinduzi Umgeni canoe marathon. At the time, I could dip a mug into the Umgeni and drink the water without fear. You take your life in your hands if you do it today. Raw sewerage, industrial waste, and the Lord knows what else is being poured into the Umzinduzi.

To say that the catchments have deteriorated would be putting it very mildly. They were unable to withstand the floods of 1987, and the whole character of the rivers has changed beyond recognition.

One memory keeps coming back to me from the 1950s, when I worked as a young game ranger in the Umfolozi Game Reserve. It is of the huge riverine forests lining the Black and the White Umfolozi Rivers. They were so full of life and such a joy to walk through. It was an experience equal to — if not much better than — visiting the great cathedrals of Europe. I learnt so much from my old Zulu friend, old Magqubu Ntombela, who used to refer to the trees as "asizabantu" — "the trees that help the people" — because in times of drought their figs sustained everybody.

Catchment destruction, the floods of 1963, and Cyclone Demoina in 1984 wiped out those riverine forests. Once, where there were deep pools in which I swam — carefully, because of crocodiles — there is now only sand.

Part of the problem, of course, is over-population. But there has also been exploitation by sometimes very rapacious industrial forces. Today, every single game reserve, nature reserve, and national park in South Africa is threatened.

Every excuse is offered for the development of areas that in fact should be sacrosanct in the true sense of that word. Every argument is advanced for the devastation of wilderness areas which should be kept in trust for our children.

A plague of weak people

We are plagued by treacherous, weak people. People who seek short-term gains to line their pockets. Weak political figures who listen to the wrong information. In my lifetime I have been involved in one desperate rearguard action after another.

Internationally, it is no different. Modern man has taken Genesis very literally and done a pretty good job. The earth's forests are being destroyed at the rate of one football field every second.

At the same time, in South Africa, exotic trees are being planted in vast quantities, in areas where they shouldn't be. They're being planted in some areas in the Drakensberg, for example, and this is affecting the water table. It's also wiping out the habitat of some of our most sensitive species, including the oribi and various wild flowers.

A huge hole is opening in the ozone layer — that seems to be beyond doubt now — and it's reducing the earth's ability to protect life from deadly ultra-violet rays.

Chemical wastes in growing volumes seep downward to poison ground water, and upward to destroy the earth's delicate balance. Living species are dying at such a rate that more than half may disappear in our lifetime. An estimate of the current extinction rate is 1 000 species a year. In the next five years the figure is likely to rise to 10 000 species a year. In the next 30 years one million species could be erased.

In 1970, there were something like 70 000 black rhino on the continent of Africa; today there are 4 000 — and more than half of them are in this country. It is only in South Africa that the black rhino population is expanding. I predict that in the next 20 years black Africa will ask us to restock their parks with black rhino as we have done with white rhino.

Diminishing returns

Mankind has become like a drug addict, needing ever-increasing doses to produce the same effect. We have lost our spiritual connection with the earth.

Some 10 000 to 15 000 years ago, when man was still a hunter-gatherer, a most terrible break with nature took place. Whereas nature had been revered, she now became an enemy. Anyone with crops had to protect them from animals and birds and insects. Whatever threatened the crop had to be eliminated.

Regrettably, in our western, Christian-dominated world, with our patriarchal attitude, there is the same urge to dominate and subdue nature; we're acting out the dark part of ourselves.

Erich Neumann, a pupil of the great psychologist, Jung, put it like this:

> Our ancient contact with nature has gone and with it has gone a profound mental energy that this symbolic action supplied. Thunder is no longer the voice of an angry god nor is lightning his avenging missile. No river contains a spirit, no tree is the life principle of a man, no snake the embodiment of wisdom, no mountain cave the home of a great demon, no voices now speak to man from the stones, the plants and the animals, nor does he speak to them believing that they can hear.

And Hermann Hess, the German poet and writer, put it in a very
beautiful nostalgic poem:

Sometimes, when a bird cries out or when the wind sweeps
through a tree or a dog howls in a far off place, I hold still and
listen a long time.

My soul turns and goes back to the place where a thousand
forgotten years ago, the bird and the blowing wind were like
me and were my brothers.

My soul turns into a tree, an animal, a cloud bank, then
changed and odd it comes home and asks me the question,
"What should I reply?"

What Herman Hess was referring to, of course, was the time
when man was still unconscious and moved across the earth in
a very harmonious way. Then came the light of consciousness,
and with it the struggle that is biblically illustrated between
Jacob and Esau.

Where to from here?

Are we going to shrink from the unimaginably difficult response
demanded by the global environmental crisis, and hope against
hope that we will not have to do anything? Or is there a reverse
process?

I don't need anyone to tell me that we will never be able to
wear skins, carry clubs, and go back and live in caves. Our
industrial age, I know, is here to stay. But with proper planning,
sensitivity, and foresight, we could work towards enhancing the
quality of our life and look for meaning beyond money.

Most importantly, we could try to live in a greater degree of
harmony with the earth and with ourselves. I believe that man
is at war with his fellow man and with nature because he is not
at peace with himself.

The destructive reality

Deep down, very deep down, we know that the course of civilisation has to be changed. We are in grave danger of destroying
the planetary ecological systems that sustain life. There is with-

out question a global awakening taking place. For the first time in our evolutionary history we know what the earth looks like from outer space, and nothing has had a greater impact upon the human mind than that.

We are able to reflect upon the planet as a whole now, and this has radically affected out thinking and our actions. The whole earth is constantly being monitored from outer space by satellites. Tiny objects the size of a matchbox can be photographed. So we are measuring the destruction of forests and we are watching the effects of soil erosion and pollution as they take place.

This is a new age, but until now insufficient national or international action has been taken.

The 1970s saw an explosion in what has become known as the Green Movement. New organisations appear every day. Governments have been challenged.

But perhaps most importantly for me, scientist after scientist to whom I speak has now come to realise that humanity has entered into a completely new relationship with the planet. This understanding is seeping through into every nation bit by bit, drop by drop. A truth is manifesting itself: if we poison the earth and destroy it we poison and destroy ourselves.

Look back, look ahead

In this modern world, we'd do well to heed the wisdom of the past. To go back to the ancient primeval world, to the ancient tribes.

The North American Indians say: "Whatever you do today you do for the seventh generation." If we followed this simple advice, there would be a much greater state of harmony between man and the world.

A major task in South Africa is to develop a clear-cut policy that makes all our proclaimed wildlands national parks, game reserves, and nature reserves sacrosanct. That policy should become law, and that law should go into the new constitution.

We don't want any mining in those areas, we don't want the army using them for weapons training or testing grounds, we don't want freeways going through them. These intrusions have got to be fought by all of us.

We desperately need more wilderness areas — both inside and outside our parks — where people can walk, ride, and canoe, away from the sights and sounds of human habitation.

I've worked with many of the "street children," and the impact of wild areas upon those young people would take me a month to explain. Nothing has been a bigger force for change in their lives than that experience.

We have other things to do, too. We have to protect our villages and bring soul back into our cities. That will take two generations, maybe more. But we've got to start thinking and feeling in the right way. Sensitivity has got to be the key word for the future.

We have to re-learn that we are part of the natural world and that the harm we do to the earth we do to ourselves. Like Icarus who tried to fly to the sun on waxed wings, we have become inflated with our technology. Let us begin again to listen with the inner ear and look with the inner eye at the ancient earth rhythms.

Part Two
VISIONS
OF THE FUTURE

In this section, five South Africans
from diverse backgrounds
and representing very different interests
talk about their visions of the new South Africa.

DAVID WILLERS

David Willers became Editor of the Natal Witness
on June 1, 1990. He has had a decidedly
international career, as a diplomat with the
Department of Foreign Affairs in Italy and Angola;
a general news, parliamentary, and diplomatic
reporter with the Cape Times; Assistant Director of
the South African Institute of International Affairs;
and London Director of the South Africa
Foundation. In his ten years with the SA
Foundation, he was instrumental in forging links
and encouraging dialogue between the South
African business community and the ANC and
other organisations.

A t the best of times, it's difficult to be a soothsayer and to forecast the future. Now, it's even more difficult. We've seen very dramatic developments since February 2. We obviously don't know what the implications will be. Only time will tell. I think, however, that there is a new sense of realism in South Africa. A great deal of euphoria surrounded the events of early 1990 — the unbanning of the ANC, the release of key people, and so on. That feeling of euphoria, which was shared worldwide, has now dissipated.

Business confidence falling

Violence on a scale rarely seen in our country's history has eroded tolerance on all sides. Business confidence has been inhibited by this violence, by the uncertainty surrounding the economic plans of a future government, and by a natural cyclical downturn in the economy together with high real interest rates. Add to this the multiplier effect on inflation of the crisis in the Gulf, and low commodity prices generally, and it becomes clear that the natural resilience of the South African economy is being severely tested under conditions of stagflation.

Labour unrest has contributed to low productivity. Taxes are extremely high and the balance of payments has been under strain. South Africa has sufficient funds to pay for little more than six or seven weeks' worth of imports.

The defence of the rand in the interests of the anti-inflation campaign has been deemed by Government to be worth the expenditure of foreign exchange. The ongoing banking freeze means that we are now in our fifth year as a capital exporting country, and there is no prospect yet that the government can afford to run a deficit on the current account.

Growth in 1990 could be negative and 1991 could show little improvement. Unemployment is very high as a result. The value of our currency is declining, not only because of the natural technical disparity between our inflation rate and that of our trading partners, but also because of the political discount. The commercial rand will be under pressure to anticipate the abolition of the financial rand in 1991.

Foreign investment and international trade

Events in Eastern Europe and deteriorating terms of trade between South Africa and traditional buyers of our raw materials have caused foreign investors to think twice about investing here.

This country has over the years provided high returns because of its assets. It's probably a good idea to remind ourselves occasionally what these assets are.

We have very good communications, excellent port facilities, sound financial institutions, good power supplies, well managed water supplies, management skills, labour, land, a good civil service, a capitalist outlook (at present), education, skills, and sound financial management on the part of the government.

Despite foreign investor reservations South Africa still does billions of dollars worth of business with the United States, Europe, and other countries of the world. There is immense potential here and everything still to play for.

Two-way trade between the United Kingdom and South Africa alone amounts to almost £2 billion a year. Similar figures can be found with respect to other countries of the European Community.

The foreign perspective

Many South Africans are depressed at the moment. All signs suggest that a liberal democracy is going to be extremely difficult to achieve in the new South Africa. However, we should bear in mind that from the perspective of, say, Europe or America, things are going reasonably well. Transition to a democratic South Africa looks possible from their point of view — without a major civil war, a flight of refugees, or economic collapse, which was the experience in so many other African countries.

At this stage, their concern is probably less with the small print of civil liberties, press freedom, and the like, than with protecting their enormous stake in people and capital in South Africa.

Low-key civil war

South Africa is in the throes of a very low-key civil conflict. Rival groups are press-ganging their supporters into joining up. Events in the townships echo our experience in Angola, and it's possible that this competition for supporters and turf will escalate into a bigger civil war in the future.

Pressure for progress on talks

How will things be going from here?

Quite clearly, it all hinges on how State President FW de Klerk finesses the political transition to majority rule.

Business confidence, property prices, foreign investment, the crime rate — all the indices by which people judge the quality of their lives — will be affected by the government's game plan. De Klerk may appear to be under less pressure now than previously. But I believe he's keenly aware that in the final analysis, market forces will be the arbiter of his progress.

The markets are imposing a time constraint on him. South Africa cannot afford to be a capital exporting country forever. At some stage the World Bank, the IMF, and bankers around the world must judge that sufficient political progress has been made to enable South Africa to start rolling over her debt again. The EC promise to lift sanctions with the repeal of the Group Areas and Land Acts is a good example.

South Africa may be under-borrowed by world standards, but still has to repay some $17 billion. Without debt extensions, and in the absence of foreign investment, we will have zero growth. Socio-economic problems will simply overwhelm the country.

Half the population is under the age of 15, squatter settlements are proliferating everywhere, health services are in decline, AIDS is a time bomb, the environment is eroding because people are chopping down trees for firewood, and so on. The problems are familiar to all of us.

As a rule of thumb, South Africa needs a billion dollars' worth of foreign direct investment a year to attain a growth rate of 5%. But without a durable political settlement fairly soon — one in which the markets can have faith and under which foreign investors will once again be prepared to risk their money — we will go into what might euphemistically be called an "African decline."

For these reasons, I don't believe Mr De Klerk can postpone a political settlement. Of course, he might judge that the economic downside is a price worth paying when set against an unacceptable political risk such as a right wing backlash or something which could precipitate a race war. But chances are that talks on the shape of new constitution will start early in 1991.

In theory, it should be possible to reach agreement in two or three days, given the precedent of Namibia. In reality, it will take longer. Government and the ANC still have to reach agreement on such issues as a constituent assembly and interim authority.

The government appears to be planning a broad alliance to oppose the ANC at the polls. A referendum on the new constitution will probably be conducted along broadly similar lines to the 1983 referendum on the tricameral parliament. Liberals on the left could decide that if whites positioned themselves in an obviously adversarial way to the ANC it would not be to their advantage; so they might vote 'no' alongside the right wing, as happened in 1983.

De Klerk can't afford delay

A White referendum might be possible by June 1992, and a general election on a one-man-one-vote basis could take place as early as September 1992. To delay any longer would place the South African economy severely at risk. Had the Gulf crisis not occurred, Mr De Klerk might have had a couple of years more to better prepare whites for majority rule. However, the Gulf crisis has placed as much of a restraint on the South African economy as sanctions have done. In other words, we've been dealt a "double whammy."

An ANC government's first moves

On the basis of recent opinion polls, the ANC might win as much as 60% of the popular vote. A new ANC government, unhampered by any sense of obligation to the white community and white business, will begin very vigorously to implement its social and economic programmes.

The economic programme is already known. Essentially it is conservative, centralist, and interventionist. A central issue — the rights of companies versus the obligations of workers, the flash point over so many years — will be transformed so that companies will have few rights and many obligations and workers will have many rights and few obligations.

Socialism and nationalisation not dead

Socialism is not dead. As a theory, it is very much alive and well. In their latest thinking, socialist theorists argue that the market economy is good at producing a surplus but bad at distributing it; thus, they say, the state should assume responsibility for "distribution through growth."

The problem is, the ANC formula for foreign investment is actually a formula for disinvestment. By allowing foreign investors to repatriate only part of their dividends, the ANC is suggesting that it places no great reliance on foreign investment as a motor for growth. Indeed, it says as much: "Domestic savings and taxation will therefore be the main source of development capital" — socialist orientation will be the watch word.

Life in a low-growth society

It's easy to predict the outcome of our remaining a low-growth society, with minimal foreign funds coming in and tight exchange control as a prime fiscal instrument.

Poverty will remain high. Technological standards will decline, thus hampering our efforts to compete in export markets. The informal sector will be unduly important. (It is not a panacea. It is not necessarily a positive development. It is often simply a means of distributing available wealth around a particular development core.)

For these and other reasons, South Africa is unlikely to be the motor for Southern Africa. Few funds will be available for regional investment. Money will be needed at home for education and housing, for health and welfare.

The good news is that conservative management of the money supply will probably keep general inflation down; so initially at least, jobs will be created.

The higher tax policy of the ANC will take the froth off property and shares. But there is no reason to anticipate a collapse.

Other changes

The "Africanisation" of South African society will be incredibly rapid, starting now.

Millions of people will move to the cities. Radio and television will change fundamentally in character. The Euro-centric emphasis in arts and education that South Africans have been so used to will make way for Afro-centrism. Crime will probably be high, as it is in other African societies with a First World/Third World structure.

US President George Bush sees South Africa becoming a bigger version of Zimbabwe — with a rather austere society and an austerely run semi-socialist economy — rather than another Kenya, with its free-wheeling markets.

The press, despite lip service to the contrary by every political party, is unlikely to be free. There is already enormous

pressure on people in the townships to conform, and newspapers
are experiencing intimidation first-hand.

The erosion of these freedoms may take some years, however, since it is the present government's clear intention to
bequeath the equivalent of Jeffersonian democracy to its succes-
sor. And because of the economic constraints on Mr De Klerk,
I don't see him easily allowing the talks to be derailed, even if
the low-key civil conflict which I have described was to escalate
into something more major.

PROFESSOR
LOUISE TAGER

Louise Tager is Honourary Professor of Law at the
University of the Witwatersrand. She was awarded
the Society of Advocates' prize as the most
outstanding LLB student in 1970. She was
appointed Professor of Law at Wits in 1978, and
from 1981 to 1985 served as Dean of the Faculty
of Law — the first woman to hold such a post in
South Africa. In 1985 she was appointed to the
Standing Committee for the Small Claims Court,
and was co-opted as a member of the Margo
Commission of Inquiry into the Tax Structure of
SA. In 1986 she was appointed to the Competition
Board, Deregulation Committee, and in 1988 she
was appointed Chairman of the Harmful Business
Practice Committee. Professor Tager has served as
Executive Officer of the Law Review Project since
1985. This project is a legal resource, funded by
the private sector, which investigates and
addresses those factors in the legislative and
administrative structure of the country which
contribute to unjust or inappropriate differences
within our society.

South Africa and South Africans are in a period of parenthesis, a period of transition. Everyone is anticipating changes in legislation, as we move away from the old apartheid system.

However, no matter how many laws we change, we are not going to achieve real change. The only way to do that is to change our attitudes. And I am not referring only to white South Africans; I am referring to *all* South Africans. It is not enough to change the statute books and abolish discrimination and racial provisions. People have to change their *thinking*.

The apartheid mentality that has been ingrained into our minds, and in the minds of our predecessors, will be around for many years after the legislation has gone. Our future hinges on how much we are able to change as individuals.

For black South Africans, living under an apartheid system has meant a certain approach to life. It has created a certain mentality. Now, it is as necessary for blacks to change as it is for whites.

Black South Africans will have to grasp the opportunities that become available as the laws change. They'll have to seize the opportunity to participate in the economy.

Paying lip service to change

We can now look ahead with a new realism that we were not able to contemplate in the past. But too many people are paying lip service to change, and they are not conducting their lives differently. Unless every South African starts participating in the changes, no change will come about.

Legacy of the past

As the economy develops and grows, it is going to offer many new opportunities, especially to black South Africans. But in order to go forward, we need to understand some of the past.

During the periods of colonialism and apartheid, a system of dependence was created, a system of hand-outs and aid. And that paternalism, although it may have been well-intended, has brought about a dependence in the black community which has inhibited people from developing fully or from reaching their potential.

People do not need paternalism. They need to find their own way through life. They need the opportunity to do so.

Fortunately, there's a very strong spirit of goodwill and entrepreneurship in this country. As laws change and restrictions are removed — and they are being removed — the opportunities that will be created in a free market economy will accelerate the development of entrepreneurship.

What should we really expect from the informal sector?

There is a tendency in South Africa to glorify the informal sector. We should realise that the informal sector is a survival economy. It has offered people a way into the economy in spite of restrictive legislation.

I fear that the word "informal" has become a euphemism for "black business." The informal sector, or informal business, does not meet the aspirations of black businessmen. People want to take part in the economy and not be labelled "informal." In any event, we must beware of glorifying the informal sector and assuming that it is an end in itself. It is a means to an end, and that end is in the highest levels of the economy.

As more black businessmen emerge — and thousands of them are doing so throughout the country — developed businesses must consider partnerships. They must find ways to share the expertise and skills that they have developed with the emerging entrepreneur.

This is particularly important in the building industry, where there are thousands of emergent black builders and contractors. They need to become part of the industry. They should not be regarded as "informal" or as "the workforce."

I would urge every white company to consider partnerships, to look for ways to bring emergent black businessmen into their operations. This is the way to share the future. It is also one way to encourage the youth to participate in the economy.

Many youngsters have asked: "Could you tell me how to start a spaza shop?" Starting a spaza shop is just a first step. It's not the ultimate. It's not where that person will want to be when he's 40 or 50, but it's a way into the economy.

The impact of deregulation

Deregulation will have a major impact on economic opportunity. The law governing trading licences has already changed, and from 1991 it will change dramatically.

But as some laws are relaxed, others will be used indirectly to control situations. We will have to be very careful that these indirect controls do not themselves impede economic development.

Much has been said about deregulation in labour-intensive industries. There are many fears. Obviously, the hard-earned rights of workers have to be protected, but at the same time we have to create jobs. Any adjustment or changes to Industrial Council agreements and labour legislation will have to be undertaken with the full participation of the trade unions.

FANYANA MAZIBUKO

Fanyana Mazibuko is Director of the University
Preparation Programme Trust and Chairman of the
Trust for Educational Advancement in South
Africa. He is also involved with the Academic
Support Programme at the University of the
Witwatersrand's Centre for Continuing Education.
From 1966 to 1977 he was a teacher, and later
vice-principal, at the Morris Isaacson High School.
He is a member of the Advisory Committee of both
the Standard Bank and Anglovaal, and Chairman
of the Impumelelo Family Resource Centre
Committee of the Johannesburg Child Welfare
Society. Throughout his career he has tackled the
shortcomings in the education system, and
attempted to help people create a sound career base.

O ur educational system is in a state of crisis. It is not able to meet even the present needs. It is going to be worse in the future.

Any analysis of our education system will of necessity be done by different people from different perspectives.

Some people will look at the provision of facilities, as has been done *ad nauseam* in this country, with blame apportioned to all and sundry.

Some people will examine the efficiency of personnel in performing their tasks. Once again, that has been done, and blame has been apportioned.

And some people will look at factors such as culture — and again, that has been done, and blame has been apportioned.

The real question is, what kind of system do we need for the future? Let's forget blaming people, because there's no time for that. Let's concentrate instead on generating solutions.

First, what is the problem?

As recently as 1988, there were some 119 027 students taking technical subjects in secondary schools and tertiary institutions combined. In contrast, 2 427 100 were doing academic courses. (In Germany, only 30% of tertiary-level students are in universities; the other 70% go into technical institutions.)

Our system is a product of South Africa's British heritage — a system that produces ladies and gentlemen who can engage in very intelligent philosophical discussion, but produce absolutely nothing.

In fact, it's worse than that. We produce these ladies and gentlemen who expect to be placed in high paying jobs, who consume a great deal — and produce absolutely nothing.

Many people now say that our economic survival rests on our ability to compete internationally through exports. But there is no chance of our being successful if we carry on turning out the kind of people we're turning out today.

The potential is there

We have the potential human resources to close the gap. We have the potential to swing things around.

In the past, as an African, one either had to make it in the six or seven professions that you were allowed into, or you were relegated to being a labourer. I hold a reference book which is stamped "Ongeskoolde arbeider" — unskilled labourer — even though I have been to university. I just didn't have any skill to show, and I hadn't studied for one of the acceptable professions. Until fairly recently, Africans were prohibited from registering as apprentices. (In 1985, there were 9 246 white apprentices, and only 666 blacks.) Because of this, there's now a great deal of resistance among blacks to technical training. So young black people are channelled into academic careers even if they do not have the aptitude or the interest.

Of the 119 027 students at technical institutions in South Africa, 86 529 are white, 15 613 are African, 8 461 are Coloured and 8 424 are Asian. In other words, whites account for 73% of students, while Africans account for just 13%.

Various factors have led to this situation. Among them were both the laws of the land and the survival strategies adopted by Africans.

Changes in the curriculum

At the moment, far too few students learn maths and science. Yet even the lowest level of technical training is impossible without these subjects.

When they enter secondary school, students should begin with an academic core of English or Afrikaans, plus mathematics and science. They should also have an elective of two other practical subjects, and a third group of subjects in the humanities.

Who'll pay for the changes?

To me, the redistribution of wealth means *redistributing the ability to generate wealth.*

To make this happen, two steps are necessary.

First, to avoid the view that redistribution means taking from those who have and giving to those who don't, we'll have to engage in a very intensive publicity campaign. We'll have to aggressively promote a new attitude towards education and training.

Second, business will have to team up with the state to provide the funds. Once again, Germany provides the example. There's a close partnership between business and government in that country to provide technical training. Some of the bigger companies actually build and run technical training centres.

A third possibility is for education to remain the responsibility of Government, but for the schools or colleges to be owned and run by various interest groups. In Sweden, for example, trade unions own schools, as do other organisations or even individuals.

The point is, we do have alternatives. We can do something constructive. We can redress the imbalances.

MERVYN KING

Mervyn King is Executive Chairman of the Frame
Group, and Deputy Chairman of Tradegro Ltd.
After a highly successful legal career, he was
appointed a Judge in the Supreme Court in 1977.
He resigned from the Bench in 1980, and is today
one of South Africa's most influential
industrialists.

The need for economic expansion from South Africa into Southern Africa, and economic pragmatism in the region, will be the forces which will determine our future economic system.

Two events played a vital role in forming Southern Africa. They were the European thrust in South Africa, started by the Dutch East India Company in the Cape, and the discovery of diamonds and gold.

Economic pragmatism dictated that expansion fostered by white entrepreneurs from South Africa should not only be tolerated, but welcomed — as it indeed was. So economic expansion and pragmatism emerged as the greatest forces in Southern Africa in the last decade of the 19th Century.

Economic pragmatism also emerged as the greatest force affecting events in South Africa in the last few decades. Let's look at a few facts.

❑ Economic pragmatism brought about the phenomenon of urbanisation in South Africa.

❑ By the year 2000 seven out of ten matriculants will be black.

❑ R7 out of every R10 spent in the Johannesburg CBD today comes out of black pockets.

❑ Economic pragmatism has driven segregation out of our education system in universities, technikons, and schools.

❑ From at least 1910 we saw attempts to segregate the South African community, but the pragmatism of economics resulted in communities becoming more and more integrated. The concept of blacks as sojourners in urban South Africa has been revealed as nothing more than Verwoerd in Wonderland.

The new reality in South Africa

The concept of Europe ignoring West Germany in planning its industrial and commercial future has an air of unreality about it. Equally unreal is the idea of Southern African states ignoring South Africa.

The reality is, we are inextricably intertwined because of South Africa's know-how and infrastructure.

❑ Botswana, Lesotho, Mozambique, and Swaziland get 35% to 100% of their electricity from South Africa.

❑ Lesotho and Swaziland get 60% to 70% of their total government revenue from the Southern African Customs Union.

❑ All Southern African states depend on South Africa to transport their goods, and they use our ports.

❑ There are 400 000 workers from Southern African states in this country.

❑ Tourism in countries such as Malawi depends on South Africa.

❑ Our neighbours depend on us for technology.

❑ The superpowers are tired of hand-outs. They don't believe in them any more. Too many African dictators have become multi-millionaires from hand-outs.

❑ First world countries have become donor-weary when it comes to Southern Africa.

❑ There is a new realisation on the part of Southern African leaders that European countries and the United States have a new agenda for hand-outs.

❑ SADCC countries have conceded that the benefits of the agreement have been more imagined than real, and that it could not be successful without South Africa.

The concept of South Africa as a platform in the structuring of Southern African economies has been widely accepted in Europe and the US. Support in principle has been received from Namibia, Lesotho, Swaziland, Mozambique, Malawi, Botswana, and now Madagascar.

Mr Ratsiraka, the Prime Minister of Madagascar, recently said: "When one is in politics, you have to face reality. At one stage it was in the best interests of my country to break relations with South Africa. We now have commercial, economic, and cultural relations with the new South Africa because it is in the best interests of Madagascar."

In short, if you destroy this economy you destroy what is left of the Southern African economy. Use South Africa's economic infrastructure and resources, and the economies of Southern Africa have a chance of being resurrected.

We can't escape global trends

Southern Africa has not escaped global trends in the last decade; nor will it do so in the 1990s. We are part of the global village.

Worldwide today, socialism is being abandoned and there's a move toward mixed economies. There's a move from statism to individualism, from central state control to deregulation and privatisation, from hand-outs to hand-ups.

How have these global trends impacted on Southern Africa so far?

Guinea introduced socialism into Southern Africa in 1959. It was followed by Tanzania, Zambia, and Mozambique.

President Chissano of Mozambique has accepted that the socialist policies started by Samora Machel have failed. The Zambian government recently took the decision to sell shares in parastatal companies in which it took a controlling interest some 25 years ago, when President Kaunda implemented his socialist policies. After 70 years of socialism, Russia now plans to evolve a market economy in 500 days.

Does South Africa need Southern Africa?

There are an estimated 35 million people in South Africa (including the homelands). Employment has to be created for these people, and to do that we have to expand our markets. The Southern African market is right on our doorstep.

The economic pragmatism of South Africa is that inflation, unemployment, population growth, and the lack of foreign capital compel us to cooperate with our neighbours. And there are many indications that this cooperation is already developing.

❑ South Africa is involved in agriculture, wildlife and nature conservation, education, training, and health projects.

❑ A Zambian Airways DC10 leaves Johannesburg twice a week on its direct flight to New York.

❑ Many students, business leaders, and politicians have had discussions with the ANC about the future of Southern Africa — not just of South Africa.

❑ The World Bank is examining the possible impact of cooperation between South Africa and the Southern African states.

Conclusion

In my view, the 1990s will see an attempt to resurrect the economies of Southern Africa by utilising the know-how and infrastructure of South Africa. There will be global recognition that regional solutions must include South Africa. And just as economic pragmatism is driving our neighbours to cooperate with us, so it will drive us to internal social and political solutions.

Economic pragmatism, and economic expansion from South Africa, will emerge as the greatest forces in Southern Africa in the last decade of the 20th Century — as they did in the last decade of the 19th Century.

Add to this perspective an economic system in South Africa which is acceptable to First World, multinational entrepreneurs, a free flow of capital back into this country, and the treasure house of national resources to which we can add value, and it's entirely possible that South Africa could become the most exciting country in the world in the 21st Century.

LAWRENCE MADUMA

Lawrence Maduma is General Secretary of the
Construction and Allied Workers Union, a
COSATU affiliate. He spent eight years at Dunlop
Flooring, then joined the South African Allied
Workers Union as an organiser for construction
and building industry workers. In 1987 the
construction unit of SAAWU merged with other
unions in the same industry to form CAWU.

In order to bring about a new South Africa with dynamic economic growth, we must first and foremost address the political situation.

It is no secret that apartheid has created imbalances in our society. Therefore we must all strive to bring about a non-racial, non-sexist democratic South Africa. Let us look at some of the factors which will bring prosperity in our country.

Economic growth

In the decade 1960 to 1970, the economy grew by an average of 5,8% a year. But in the 1970s it declined — to 1,4% by 1989.

Sanctions and resistance to apartheid have resulted in a withdrawal of confidence by many potential foreign and domestic investors. External factors such as a rising oil price, a low gold price, and a downturn in the world economy in the same period have also had a serious effect. Today, we see the country plunged into an economic crisis.

However, the government is taking positive steps to create grounds for a negotiated political settlement. Hopefully, sanctions will soon be lifted. Then a future democratic non-racial government can face the problem of reconstructing the economy.

In that process it will need the full support of employers. Presently the business community fears nationalisation as part of a mixed economy. We believe this is not a new phenomenon.

When the National Party took power, it nationalised some key industries to generate sufficient funds for its programme. It is along those lines that we believe nationalisation should be considered in a post-apartheid system.

However, we are not dogmatic about this approach, as long as opponents of this view can offer a more acceptable proposal to the majority of the poor masses. It will also be necessary for a new government to invite investors and give them some incentive to encourage them.

Stabilising the economy

Industrial peace should be promoted by a future government to ensure that investors are not frightened away. There should be an investment code accepted by both employers and unions as major players in the economy. Employers should learn to live with unions. Hence it is imperative that unions draft a workers' charter which will be attached to a future constitution. This would serve as a catalyst in the event of disputes. Employers would have to respect International Labour Organisation (ILO) conventions.

Workers — blacks in particular — should be drawn into production planning now so as to prepare for future economic growth. That would promote production quality.

But such an aim will never be accomplished while companies are hesitant about training workers. Companies should establish industry training funds. Workers should be re-cycled in each industry to curtail increasing unemployment. This would also slow the flow of skilled immigrants.

Redistribution of wealth

A non-racial democratic government will have to address imbalances in wages, unemployment, education, housing, and so on. Government will have to inject more funds to welfare and social projects, with the aim of uplifting poor people.

Such endeavours should be a joint venture between government and employers. The resulting increase in buying power would create a great demand for local commodities such as food, clothing, building materials, etc. Then companies would have to employ more workers in every industry.

We also urge companies to address the issue of housing for their workers. Such initiatives should involve the unions in the relative industry.

Organisations such as BIFSA should encourage all their affiliates to adopt centralised bargaining. These federations should address irregularities taking place in Industrial Councils, and attract other parties to participate at industry level.

It is also our desire to see employers support the development of small-scale industries as cooperatives. Again, this would help alleviate unemployment.

The land question

Until recently there have been forced removals of blacks from their original homes. This dispossession has confined them to "reserves" comprising only 13% of the country's land.

We expect a future government to address this problem so as to promote the equal distribution of wealth. Such redistribution should consider the interest of the people at large. People should be able to till land, and be assisted by the state with modern implements and seed.

Regional economic growth

Post-apartheid South Africa will have to promote economic relations with its neighbours. A future government will have to address regional imbalances and the damage done to Southern African economies by apartheid destabilisation.

A new government should be able to promote dynamic and mutually beneficial cooperation and development. These measures would alleviate regional unemployment.

In conclusion

We must all learn to live together and create proper mechanisms to resolve our differences.

MANAGEMENT TITLES FROM JUTA

GETTING IT RIGHT — The Manager's Guide to Business Communication

ADEY & ANDREW

This work is more an introduction to business practice than a book about theoretical communication. Management, marketing, advertising, and industrial relations are approached from the perspective of business communication. Each chapter has a summary of concepts and terms, as well as case studies that test the understanding of these concepts. The syllabi of the diplomas of various professional institutes, including that of the Communication Course of the Diploma in Business Administration as examined by the SA Institute of Management, are covered.

COMMUNICATING FOR CHANGE — A Guide to Managing the Future of South African Organisations

A D MANNING

Communicating for Change is based upon this simple idea: 'Business has a serious responsibility to remain viable, create wealth, and generate jobs and opportunities for personal growth; to sensitise people to the need for change; and to help them learn new behaviours and thus bring about change.' This book not only shows the reader how to increase profits, but it also addresses the all-important changes in our South African society and shows how a climate for change can be created in every workplace.

WORLD CLASS! — Strategies for Winning with Your Customer

A D MANNING

Tony Manning, one of South Africa's leading management consultants and an expert in customer care, believes that obsessive attention to your customer is the surest way to boost business profits. But, he says, training 'front line' people is not enough. Continuous improvement of everything is vital for success. This book helps managers to create an holistic attack strategy and the market-focused culture that it needs. It is the first total blueprint for success in the competitive business arena—a practical, step-by-step approach to reinventing the organisation; complete with charts, questionnaires, workshop agenda and planning guides.

MARKETING MANAGEMENT

MARX & VAN DER WALT

Written to suit South African conditions, the style of this text is easy, while figures and tables are used liberally to explain complicated concepts. While characterised by a practical approach, the content is scientifically founded. The twenty chapters are divided into four parts. The first is a general introduction providing a broad perspective; the second deals with the marketing environment; the third with marketing decisions and the fourth part, including topics such as the product life cycle, marketing warfare, strategic marketing, product portfolio etc, deals with the integrated marketing strategy. This work is also available in Afrikaans.

ASSESSING MANAGERIAL COMPETENCE

HERMANN SPANGENBERG

This book is based upon research results and years of experience which show that the tasks and roles of managers at various organisational levels differ substantially, calling for different success criteria and, consequently, differences in the required competencies. Competencies in themselves are complex, differing in type and level, and this work should prove to be indispensable in the assessment of the potential of managers and supervisors.